Ernest Seyd

The decline of prosperity: its insidious cause and obvious remedy

Ernest Seyd

The decline of prosperity: its insidious cause and obvious remedy

ISBN/EAN: 9783337085919

Printed in Europe, USA, Canada, Australia, Japan

Cover: Foto ©Suzi / pixelio.de

More available books at **www.hansebooks.com**

THE

DECLINE OF PROSPERITY:

ITS

INSIDIOUS CAUSE AND OBVIOUS REMEDY.

"The value of money has been settled, by general consent, to express our wants and our property, as letters were invented to express our ideas; and both these institutions, by giving a more active energy to the powers and passions of human nature, have contributed to multiply the objects they were designed to represent."—*Gibbon's Decline and Fall of the Roman Empire*, Chapter 9.

"The quantities of Gold and Silver procurable will prove no more than sufficient to meet the exigencies of an enormously increased population, and an augmenting commerce and industry.—Providence seems to have originally adjusted the relative values of the precious metals, and the fact that their relations have remained the same for ages will survive all theories."—*Sir Roderick Murchison.*

BY

ERNEST SEYD, F.S.S.

LONDON:

EDWARD STANFORD, 55 CHARING CROSS, S.W.

1879.

LONDON:

PRINTED BY THE CIVIL SERVICE PRINTING AND PUBLISHING COMPANY, LIMITED,
8 SALISBURY COURT. FLEET STREET, E.C.

CONTENTS.

APPENDIX.

ADDITIONAL.

THE DECLINE OF PROSPERITY:

ITS INSIDIOUS CAUSE AND OBVIOUS REMEDY.

CHAPTER I.

The Decline of Prosperity affects the interest of all classes.—Its real cause is Legislation in regard to Metallic Money.—The Contraction of the Metallic Currency of the world.—This publication is designed to serve as a Handbook to the question.

The decline of prosperity in England and other countries, which the signs of the present times appear to indicate, is a subject in which every member of the human family has a deep personal interest. There have been periods of so-called crisis, affecting commerce and finance, but these lasted only a short time, were followed by quick recovery, and affected special branches of trade and industry. The present depression, however, has continued for nearly six years, in the successive stages of its steady decline, and its influence has spread over all classes. The hope that there will soon be an improvement has no solid grounds; the current allegations as to the reasons of the falling off also appear to be baseless. The real fact is that *one main cause exists*, to which the whole evil may be traced.

It is the object of this publication to bring this main cause before the reader; but when it is here at once mentioned that the cause is connected *with metallic money,* or rather with the *laws affecting its use,* many people may feel disinclined to give their attention to so dry and intricate a theme. Nevertheless, an earnest appeal must here be made to all, landowners, property holders, men devoted to science and art, bankers, manufacturers, merchants, and tradesmen. The working classes have an interest in the question, because it exercises a fatal influence on their well-being. (See Appendix page 93.)

The depression of trade and industry has been ascribed to many causes, among these "overtrading," "overproduction," "high living," "growing inferiority of our manufactures," "strikes of workmen and drunkenness," belong to our supposed *internal* shortcomings. Then, "cycles of trade," "cessation of loans to foreigners," "foreign wars," finally, "foreign competition," and "protection in foreign countries," are alleged to be the *external* causes. Neither individually nor collectively do the reasons given cover the question. Some of them are irrelevant, some counteract each other, and altogether, none are of such an unusual or novel nature as to account for the sudden change from progress to continued steady decline. Above all, the depression of trade is not confined to this country, but is universal.

The *true cause* of the abnormal depression of trade is *the contraction of the metallic currency by "human" law,* the so-called "demonetisation of silver."

B

In explaining the subject in these pages, it is assumed that the reader is fairly acquainted with the character of money and its relations to "value" and "commodities"; further, that he is free from any speculative tendency to make the world happy by "more bank notes," and kindred suggestions as to substitutes. For whatever may be the merits or demerits of what can and has been done in that direction, here we are concerned with a matter which is distinct in itself, "the contraction of the metallic stock of money in the world by changes in legislation." That, independently of every other consideration, this must have an almost commanding influence on the trade and prosperity of the world is instinctively felt by many people, and they may conceive that this concerns the foundation upon which all superstructures are formed. Here in England there has been no alteration in legislation on metallic money since 1816, and as these changes have taken place abroad, many Englishmen not already acquainted with the matter will therefore ask: "what have we to do with it?" The question is all the more pertinent because the legislation adopted by foreign states follows certain principles of our own, and it has been the subject of a fierce economical controversy. (See Appendix, page 87.)

The consideration of the subject here in England is therefore liable to be impeded by prejudice; but it will here be shown why the imitation of our English system was not suitable to the circumstances of other nations, and *above all why this has so seriously affected the commerce of England.* The immense importance of the whole matter cannot strike the reader until he has gained an insight into certain elements involved in it. When these are clearly before him, the salient points of the case can be developed, so that he will easily understand their bearing. He may then also find that the inherent abstruseness of matters of currency is by no means as formidable as is sometimes supposed. All this is said to encourage the reader to enter into the consideration of the cause, for it is upon the British public and its government that the decision for good or evil depends, as will be shown in the course of the book. The design is that it should serve *as a handbook*, and for this purpose an unstudied style, as well as the occasional repetition of leading features, must be excused by those already better versed in the subject than the general reader.

CHAPTER II.

The Distinction between full "Legal Tender Money" and "Subsidiary Coinage."

The first point to which the attention of those new to the subject must be directed is the difference between so-called *full legal tender money* and *subsidiary coinage.* Most people imagine that the coins current in the various countries derive their value from the quantity of precious metal which they contain. This is true for "full legal tender" coins, which constitute the great bulk of all metallic coinages. But the lesser portion, the "subsidiary" coins, used for *change,* are of an inferior kind, the difference between their metallic and current value being maintained by the force of the law.

Full legal tender coin is so called, because the creditor must accept it when tendered, for any amount due to him, however large it may be. Such coin is made of gold or of silver, as the laws of various countries determine. The State mints are bound to coin all good bullion brought to them by the public, into legal tender coins, charging nothing in some countries, or making a small charge in others, for doing so. They return the coin in exact agreement with the laws regulating its weight and fineness, so that when new pieces are melted down, they are again of the same mint value as bullion. Such coin can accordingly, like uncoined bullion, be sent from one nation to another for conversion into the other's coinage. But this depends, to some extent, upon the choice which the nations have made as regards the two metals for use as legal tender. In England, for instance, gold only is legal tender; in France, both gold and silver are used as such; in Germany silver was, in India silver is, the only "real" money. In England, the law says: One ounce of standard gold shall be coined into £3 17s. 10½d. In France the kilogramme of 900 fine gold is minted into 3,100 francs of gold pieces, the kilogramme of 900 fine silver into 200 francs of 5fs. silver pieces. In Germany the law was: 30 thalers are coined from the mint pound of pure silver. The Indian rupee weighs one tola, or 180 troy grains, containing 165 grains pure silver. All legal tender gold and silver coins in other countries are freely coined on the same principle; the respective methods of stating the coinage laws differ only in terms, and the relations between the coins find expression in the rate of exchange.

Subsidiary coinage consists of silver pieces of inferior quality or short weight, and of copper (or bronze, and in some States nickel). Copper coinages, for instance, usually contain only one-third of their nominal value in actual metal. Such a coinage is nevertheless maintained in circulation at its nominal value, in virtue of the law whereby its tender is limited to a small definite number of pieces (in England twelve), for any one payment. For if anyone were to coin good copper pieces indistinguishable in weight and form from those issued by the mint, he could not dispose of anything like a sufficient number to earn a day's wages without immediately being detected. The object of this arrangement is obvious, and it establishes a distinction in principle as well as in practice between subsidiary coins and full legal tender coins. Under these conditions the amount of copper current is limited; and it may be stated that the percentage of copper or bronze coin in a country rarely exceeds 1½ per cent of the total value of the circulation.

Subsidiary coins are also made of silver, but the use of silver as a material for coins of this class is of comparatively modern origin. It began by the introduction of pieces of low denomination, of the value of about 3d., into which some silver was introduced to make them lighter. (See Appendix, page 59.) And a great majority of the nations either confined the issue of these pieces to values not exceeding 3d., or kept their whole silver currency at its full legal value, until in 1816, England reduced all her silver issues to the level of subsidiary or "token" coins. England, however, remained almost alone in this monetary policy until 1872.—When such subsidiary silver pieces are melted down they do not realise their value in metal. They differ from the full valued silver coins by about 10 per cent. They cannot be exported for re-coinage elsewhere, because of this loss. They are not coined for private account, but at the option of the State, which retains the profit of their issue. They are under "*limited tender,*" and nobody is obliged to receive more than £2 in any one payment. Now if it should be asked why the State can take this profit of 10 per cent., and why it could not take more, the answer is this: any manufacturer, other than the mint, might make the same coin. But as the margin is but 10 per cent., without counting the cost of coining, it would not pay him to run the risk. The coin being *tender only to £2*, he could not pay it away to banks and the wholesale trade without being speedily found out; and retail purchases, without reference to the trouble of getting rid of a sufficient quantity, would involve far larger losses on re-sale. In fact the case is similar to that alluded to above in reference to copper. On the other hand, were it not for the check imposed by the possibility of private coiners making a profit by coining good silver pieces, the State would, no doubt, be happy to make larger profits, by using still lower quality of metal for subsidiary silver coin. Indeed it will be seen that the present system of fair metallic subsidiary token or silver coinage exists to a great extent on a kind of sufferance; for if the difference between real metallic and enforced current value should be made, or should become, larger, it could not be upheld without entailing the dangers above pointed out.

The foregoing general description of the state of the currencies of the world refers to the period up to 1870. And at that time, among the gold and silver pieces used by various nations may be mentioned—

FULL LEGAL TENDER COINS.
Gold, full metallic value.
The English Sovereign.
„ „ Half Sovereign.
„ French 20 Franc Piece and its gold subdivisions.
„ American Eagle and its gold multiples,
and other foreign gold coin that need not be specified.

Silver, full metallic value.
The French Five Franc Piece.
„ Various Dollars.
„ German Thalers.
„ Dutch Florins.
„ Austrian „
„ Indian Rupees, &c., &c.

LIMITED LEGAL TENDER COINS.
Subsidiary Silver Coins or Tokens.
The English Five Shilling Piece, with the Half Crown, Florin, and sub-divisions.
The French Two Franc Piece and its sub-divisions.
The German one-twelfth Thaler and sub-divisions.
and other foreign coins of lesser importance.

In fact, in England the so-called *gold valuation, i.e.*, gold monometallism, prevails, and all our silver coinage is under limited tender as " tokens."

In France the *gold and silver valuation, i.e.*, bimetallism, is in existence.

In Germany *silver monometallism* prevailed, with a slight admixture of gold.

In India the *silver valuation, i.e.*, pure silver monometallism, was in 1870, and still is in force.

In those countries which have adopted gold monometallism the proportion of silver coinage is limited to a small amount.

In the States where bi-metallism is the law, the proportions in which the two metals enter into the currency more nearly approach equality.

In the States where silver monometallism is the law, the great bulk of the circulation consists of silver coin of full metallic value.

In the year 1870, now under consideration, there were in use in the world :—

In full legal tender gold money ... £750 millions.

In full legal tender silver money ... 590 ,,

And in subsidiary silver tokens ... 60 ,,

The difference between full legal tender and full metallic coin, whether of gold or of silver, in contradistinction to subsidiary and limited tender " token " coinage, must always carefully be borne in mind.

CHAPTER III.

The Contraction of the Metallic Money in the World by Legislation, or the " Demonetisation of Silver," generally indicated.

The preceding chapter will now serve to indicate what is meant by the " demonetisation " of silver. The proposition is made that all nations should adopt gold only, and abandon the use of silver, as legal tender money, employing the latter only for " tokens." Presuming for the moment that this were, or *must* be done, the consequence would be that by far the greater mass of silver must disappear from circulation. A token coinage is necessarily restricted in amount. When the subsidiary silver pieces belong to a silver system, the legal tender silver itself performs the functions of change, and only a small amount of tokens, say from 3 to 4 per cent on the general circulation, is required ; the same is the case where both gold and silver are legal tender. In the case of the gold valuation, in which *all* the silver coins are under the limitation, the proportion becomes larger, say equals 15 per cent. on the circulation of full legal tender money ; it cannot, however, exceed that proportion. Now if the £750 millions of gold which existed in 1870 are made the only legal tender, and the proportion of silver token coinage that can circulate with them be taken as high as 20 per cent., or at £150 millions, an amount of £500 millions of silver now in use as legal tender coin would have to be given up; to be defaced, or melted down into bars, and sold as " metal " for what they would fetch for any other purpose than money. The small proportion of subsidiary silver coinage thus to remain would require but small yearly additions, consequently the annual supplies of silver bars from mines could not in future be " turned into money" or become "monetised." Further, the use of silver bullion as security for the issue of bank notes would have to cease. Silver being thus forcibly *deposed* by law, deliberately *discarded* for the future, and *discredited*, the term " *demonetisation* " best applies to the whole proceeding. And if any State which has already so demonetised silver should retrace its steps and again adopt it as full legal tender, the word " re-monetisation " fully describes the process. It may be remarked that in 1858, Mr. Cobden, who translated M. Chevalier's book hinting at the possible " demonetisation of gold," made use of the term, and as others have since incorporated it into the English language, it may be accepted as a proper word to use in discussing the subject.

It has already been stated that this subject involves a long-standing controversy
—the so-called " Battle of the Standards." It is not the purpose of this treatise to
renew this dispute here ; but, in the Appendix to follow, a general indication of its
origin and nature will be given. (See Appendix page 87.) Nevertheless, throughout
this treatise occasional allusion will be made to what is done in England, by way of
comparison, and therein lies the difficulty pointed at in the first chapter of this
publication. Here in England it is especially difficult to obtain popular recognition
for the subject; for, in reality, the proposition to demonetise silver means that
other nations should follow England's example. That is, of course very flattering, as
it would seem, to our own institutions. It also happens that, for some time before 1870,
the " economical " tendency of a certain financial school was in favour of the
extension of the English system. A minority of writers, however, although they
conceded that the gold valuation was seemingly successful for England, were of the
opinion that its extension to other countries was fraught with the sad results on the
trade of the world—and that of England particularly—which we now witness.
Germany, however, in 1872 followed the example of England. As yet, Germany
alone has made an effective change, for reasons which will be given ; but several
other nations have made preparations to do the like. That this partial action has
already led to evil consequences, is now patent to many persons. It is the object of
this treatise concisely to set forth the grounds upon which they have arrived at that
conclusion, and to point out the only possible and infallible remedy for restoring
commercial prosperity. The reader is therefore requested to look upon comparisons
between the English and other monetary systems, not as derogatory to his own
country, but as necessary for the explanation of the general problem involved. The
" international " bearing of the matter will be found to influence England's interests
in an overwhelming manner. In order to show how the present position has been
brought about, it is necessary that in the next chapters the state of matters before
1870 should first be more clearly defined.

CHAPTER IV.

*The State of Matters in the Metallic Monetary Arrangements of the World in 1870,
as illustrated by the four principal leading systems.*

In *England*, gold only is coined into full legal tender money, no full legal tender
silver coins whatever are allowed. The whole of our silver coinage is subsidiary, from the
5s. piece downwards, and is " over-valued." A new gold sovereign contains 20s. worth
of gold; but 20s. in English silver coin, when melted down and sold at the price of silver,
of, say 60d. per ounce, only yield about 18s. 2d. At 50d. per ounce they only
give 15s. 2d. Most people, who have hitherto believed in the unimpeachable character
of British coin, are not aware of this ; but although our florins and the rest of our
silver coins look good, and are of fine quality, they contain so much *less silver ;* in
fact they are coined at the arbitrary value of 66d. per ounce, which has always been
a rate higher than the current price of silver in the market. The object of giving
to the silver coin this artificial value, was ostensibly that of preventing its export ;
the issue was confided to the charge of the Government, so as to avoid redundancy ;
and the limited tender forcibly lessened the use of silver. The three restrictions thus

provided have the effect of confining the use of silver in England to within a narrow range, and more than the proportions indicated below cannot be brought into circulation. The question whether this forcible limitation of silver is expedient in the interests of internal trade is reserved. (See Appendix, page 59.)

Gold being thus the only legal tender, *England* is the leading representative of

The gold valuation (or gold monometallism).

In 1870 there were in circulation about £105 millions of gold coin, with an average of, say £25 millions of gold bullion in the Bank of England, together therefore :—

in full legal tender gold ... ... £130 millions

and in subsidiary silver tokens ... 16½ ,,

equal to, say 12½ per cent. on gold. There is besides the usual proportion of copper coin of about £1¾ millions.

In France, in 1870, both gold and silver coins of full legal tender and full metallic value are in use, the 20 frs. gold piece, and its divisions, as well as the 5 frs. silver piece. Both these descriptions melt down to frs. 3,100 of gold and frs. 200 of silver per kilogramme 900 fine respectively. Formerly all the smaller silver coins were of full metallic value, but since 1867 the pieces from the 2 frs. downwards have been made subsidiary by the reduction of their quality to 835 fine. Although the system of subsidiary silver coinage has thus also been introduced into France, yet its distinction from the English system will be recognised. The French law maintains the silver 5 frs. piece as full legal tender, and with a full metallic value, so that the silver coinage of France has *pro tanto* a degree of expansiveness which is absent in England; there is, consequently, plenty of sound silver for the internal intercourse, and the proportion of actual debased coin of 2 frs. and below is moderate. France is the country which has hitherto acted as the mediator between the two opposing systems, and both gold and silver being legal full tender, *France* is the representative type of

The gold and silver valuation (bi-metallism).

Including the bullion in the Bank of France there were in the country :—

in full legal tender gold ... ... £240 millions.

in full legal tender silver ... ... 90 ,,

and in subsidiary silver pieces ... 9 ,,

the latter amounting to less than 3 per cent. on the whole. There are also about £4 millions, or 1¼ per cent., of copper-bronze coin.

(The reader is reminded that this statement refers to the year 1870. Before 1848 the proportion of silver had been larger; from 1848 to 1870 gold predominated, and since then the Franco-German War has deprived France of a great deal of her currency, which at this time has again been recovered. The year 1870 is therefore here chosen because it is the most convenient one for showing the state of matters previous to the change in 1872.)

In *Germany*, up to 1870, silver only was full legal tender. Besides home-made thalers and florins, many foreign silver-pieces, five francs, Dutch and Austrian florins, &c. circulated. Besides the gold crowns and older pieces, gold coins of various nations were used; but excepting their own silver pieces none of these coins were of legal tender, they were "commercial" money, and fluctuated in value and quantity. The average amount of these miscellaneous gold coins was about 20 per cent. on the amount of silver. The coinage of subsidiary silver only began with the pieces of the value of about 3d. downwards, (See Appendix, page 59) and its total in 1872 did not exceed £3½ millions. The full valued silver money amounted to about £95 millions. Of this nearly £32 millions were foreign, French, Dutch, Austrian, &c. pieces, since exported. Of the balance Germany has probably now sold two-thirds, and may have £20 millions left. The statements put forward as to a lesser quantity of silver in Germany in 1870 are wrong, it is even likely that there was more than is here given. Germany is also a silver-producing country to the extent of about £1¼ per annum. The floating quantity of gold crowns and foreign gold coins was about £19 millions. *Germany* thus represented the type of

The *silver valuation* (silver monometallism).

modified by the use of *gold as commercial money*, and in 1870 had in use:—

in full tender and full valued silver	...	£95	millions.
in commercial gold money	...	...	19	,,
and in subsidiary change...	...	...	3½	,,

the last equal to about 3 per cent. on the whole circulation. The change from silver to gold in Germany since 1870 will be referred to later on.

In India silver alone is full legal tender. Gold, during the present century, never obtained a footing in India. The gold mohur did not answer, because it was an impracticable coin. At the bi-metallic rate it was worth 15½ rupees, but the Government seems to have had an aversion to adopt this rate. If in 1834, when the present rupee was established, a gold piece of exactly 10 rupees had been provided for, in the proportion of 1 to 15½, India might have retained a fair amount of gold. All the current legal tender silver coin in India is of full metallic value, down to the smallest division of the rupee; so that a subsidiary coinage does not exist, although for practical purposes the lowest pieces may be looked upon as fractional. The imports of silver into India far exceed the coinage and the supposed existing amount of coin. Some controversy as to the amount of "bangles" and hoarded silver bars exists, but the amount for monetary purposes in India and its dependencies was not less than £200 millions in 1870. *India*, therefore, represents

The *pure silver valuation* (or silver monometallism)

and the amount of currency and bullion can be stated as:—

in full legal tender silver	...	...	£200	millions.
in subsidiary silver coin	...	...	——	,,

The copper coinage of India amounts to about £3 millions, equal to 1½ per cent. on the total circulation.

The four systems here described are the leading types, to each of which a group of other nations was attached, so that on balance, the monetary arrangements of the nations of the world produced a certain equilibrium, in virtue of which the concurrent and equal use of gold and silver was firmly established. It will be noted that no reference is here made to Bank notes. In the metallic States the paper currency is well covered by bullion, which has been included in the figures given. The States under depreciated paper issue have but an indirect influence upon the *de-facto* equilibrium.

CHAPTER V.

The Equilibrium established all over the World by the Four Leading Systems in 1816.— The Groups of Nations with their Populations.—The Quantities of, and the Steadiness of Value between, Gold and Silver up to 1872.

A brief outline of the history of metallic money will now show how these groups were formed. From time immemorial gold and silver have been used in weight as "bullion," or in the shape of full-valued "coin" as full legal tender money, in fair general agreement. Although the relative proportions between the value of gold and silver, as fixed by law, varied in different ages (See Appendix, page 82), and the national systems diverged in some measure, the aggregate of monetary legislation in the world secured the equal use of both metals as full legal tender-money. In 1816, however, England adopted the exclusive gold valuation. For some years previous to 1816, England had been using depreciated paper currency, and it was easier for her to adopt an entirely new system. (See Appendix, page 59). England, therefore, was the first country to demonetise silver; although in reality at the time she had no real stock to sell. Indeed, her action not only created no disturbance in the general aggregate, but tended rather to affirm the use of gold in the world. For although France had given to gold a fixed mint price in the bi-metallic system some years before, silver up to 1816 had been the legally predominant element. Independently, therefore, and whether the theory of the so-called single standard was involved or not, there can be no doubt that, from an international point of view, the gold valuation in England has been thoroughly successful. In fact, since 1816, the world thus became divided into these four distinct groups, and the equilibrium thus established was maintained until 1872.

In the table now submitted the nations marked with an * have no fully effective, or only a nominal system; those marked † are under depreciated paper issue. Further details on the actual condition of each will be found on pages 48 to 51 in the Appendix.

TABLE SHOWING THE VALUATIONS OF THE NATIONS IN 1870 AND 1871 UNDER EACH OF THE FOUR GROUPS. POPULATIONS STATED IN MILLIONS AND DECIMALS (00,000 OMITTED).

Gold system.	Pop.	Bi-metallic system.	Pop.	Silver system.	Pop.	Silver system (pure).	Pop.
United Kingdom	32,0	France	36,2	Germany	41,1	China ...	425,0,
Portugal*	4,0	Belgium	5,1	Holland	3,7	India	
Turkey†	27,0	Switzerland	2,7	Denmark	1,8	Settlements	
Persia*	4,4	Italy†	26,8	Sweden	4,3	Islands	195,0,
Australia	2,0	Spain*	16,4	Norway	1,7	&c.	
Cape ...	1,4	Greece†	1,4	Austria†	36,0		
Canada*	3,0	Roumania*	4,0	Russia†	76,0		
Brazil†	10,2	United States†	38,6	Egypt ...	4,6		
Argentine†	1,8	Colombia†	2,9	Mexico	9,2		
		Venezuela	1,6	West Indies ...	0,6		
		Chili ...	1,9	Bolivia†	1,8		
		Uruguay†	0,4	Ecuador†	1,3		
		Paraguay†	1,2	Peru† ...	3,4		
		Japan ...	33,0	Central America†	2,6		
Total ...	85,8	Total ...	142,2	Total ...	268,0	Total ...	620,0,

With regard to this table it is important to notice that the enormous numerical superiority of the silver-using people does not affect the validity of the above remarks on the equilibrium between gold and silver. Owing to the superiority of civilization, higher prices, and other causes, far more currency in proportion is required in the United Kingdom, say, than in China. And the same holds good in a less degree in other cases. The international equilibrium in fact depends on the respective Population, Prices, and Amount of Currency, in the various states of the world, *taken together*.

On page 69 of the Appendix an account is given of the production of gold and silver in the world, and of the amount of metallic money in use from time to time, to which reference may be made.

In 1848 there existed, apart from the use in jewellery, utensils, and other purposes, £400 millions of gold and £590 millions of silver money. Between 1848 and 1870 the Californian and Australian and other mines added £350 millions of gold. The total production was of course larger, but making allowance for what was used for other purposes, and on the most careful review of what had been actually coined, recoined, and exchanged, the £350 millions represent the addition. The addition of silver money amounted to about £60 millions. The production of this metal also was larger and even more than £60 millions were coined within the period. But as a great deal of silver bars and coin went to the East, where some portion has been melted down and is hoarded, a careful comparison between Indian and European coinages appears to give this as a nett result.

The £750 millions of gold and the £650 millions of silver money, together £1,400 millions, in 1870 and 1871 were divided among the four groups as follows:—

AMOUNT OF METALLIC MONEY IN THE WORLD IN 1870-71.

(in millions sterling.)

| | FULL LEGAL TENDER. | | TOKENS. |
	Gold.	Silver.	Subsidiary Silver.
Gold systems	£170,	£14,	£27,
Bi-metallic systems ...	360,	131,	21,
Silver systems	123,	201,	11,
Silver systems (pure) ...	30,	240,	—
Not accounted for ...	67,	5,	—
Total millions ...	£750,	£591,	£59,

The supplies and coinages from 1871 to the present year will be added later on. It will be noticed that a certain amount of legal tender silver is given under gold systems; this is due to the defective or paper States, where various foreign silver coins are used. The proportion of legal tender silver in the bimetallic countries would be larger but for the number of their silver pieces current elsewhere. The proportion of gold in silver States seems larger than that taken for Germany, because in several South-American and other States, our own, French, American, and other gold coins were made use of. Even in some of the pure silver States some gold must be allowed for. The proportion of subsidiary coinage would be larger if the fractional full metallic coin of certain States were placed in that category. (With these exceptions, this statement corresponds to one furnished to the Committee on silver in 1876[*] by the writer.)

Taking these figures as broadly representing the *status quo* in 1870 and 1871,

---

[*] See Report of Silver Committee 1876, p. 7.

it will easily be perceived that they *afforded a natural equilibrium*, in which both gold and silver found full employment among the four groups of nations. The stock, accumulated from time to time, was always in full use in internal and international commerce and exchanges. All the fresh supplies of gold and silver, varying considerably in amount with the discoveries of new mines, became incorporated with the world's circulation. The *prices of gold and silver in foreign countries*, after making allowance for charges of conveyance and mintage either way, *corresponded*, in their respective measures for weights and coinage, *with the £3 17s. 10½d. per ounce standard for gold, and the average rate of* 60⅞ *pence for the ounce of standard silver in England.* (See Appendix, page 73.)

CHAPTER VI.

The Equilibrium destroyed in 1872.—The Fall in Silver.—The American Supplies and German Sales have but an indirect effect on the price.—Useless Suggestions for employing more Silver for Plate.—Supposed Effect on Silver-Mining.—The Loss on Plate and Currency.—The main question remaining.

The equilibrium was thus maintained, until, in 1872, Germany, having received £200 millions of war indemnity from France, suddenly resolved to abandon and sell her silver and take to gold, thus utterly upsetting the previously existing equilibrium. *From the moment that Germany commenced to carry out the change, silver fell in value, and the depression of trade set in.* The term equilibrium is used purposely to indicate that, unless the proceeding taken by Germany is counteracted, there will be a steady downward course. The motives which led the Germans to demonetise silver, and the question of remonetisation, will be considered later on; for it is expedient here first to clear the ground of certain suggestions which would be naturally started by those beginning to reflect upon *the fall in the price of silver.* So far, between 1873 and 1879, from its international rate of 60⅞d. per ounce, it has declined to, say 50 pence, or by about 18 per cent. It may again vary in price, up or down, but the general indications are in the downward direction.

Why has the price of silver fallen?

Many people ascribe the fall exclusively to the greater supply of mines, by way of natural consequence; but if the history of the production of the precious metals, and their relative value, is investigated (See Appendix, pages 69 to 87), it will be found that in previous times the divergencies between the production of gold and silver were much more considerable, without causing any disturbance whatever in the relative value of the two metals. Next follow the attempts which have been made to ascribe the fall to the sales of that metal by Germany. Within the last two years America and Germany have sent less silver than before, yet, nevertheless, silver has fallen. The imports of silver from the United States into England in 1873 were £6 millions, in 1877 they were £2,700,000. In the first three months of 1877 Germany sent £1,300,000; in the same period in 1878 £1,500,000; in the first three months of 1879 only £260,000. Now, whether the American miners wait for better prices to resume active operations in certain poor mines now standing still, as for a time they are able to do, or the Germans suspend sales until they can get a higher rate, the fact that during the last two years much less silver has been offered for sale than in the period before 1877 is undoubted. And this is a feature quite apart from the diminished demand for the East. So long as the old equilibrium lasted, the supplies of gold and silver to any amount were always freely absorbed. The extra supplies of silver from American mines do not amount to £6 millions more than the customary general yield per annum, or 1 per cent on the stock of silver. In truth, the *real cause of the fall of the price in silver, is the enforced cessation of the demand resulting from its demonetisation, by mistaken legislation;* the additional supplies having only a small share in the consequent decline. If the demonetisation of silver had not been brought about by the vagaries of the law, as indicated, the American and all other supplies would still be absorbed, as all new metal has been before. (See Chap. VIII. and Appendix, page 73.)

To what extent can silver be used for other purposes than money ?

The most ordinary suggestion is : " That silver should be used more extensively for plate and ornaments; that this would contribute to uphold its price." In England the consumption of silver for plate is less than £200,000 per annum. From the official returns of the Goldsmiths' Hall, at least one-fourth must be deducted as old plate remade, and a great deal of old plate is melted down for bullion. The consumption for small unmarked articles, and electro-plating (for which broken up pieces and strippings of old goods also serve), may raise the entire use of fresh silver here to £300,000 to £350,000 a year. England being the richest country for plate and plating, and exporting to her colonies and elsewhere, the rest of the civilised world may use from say £1½ to £2 millions. In India the consumption for bangles and for hoarding cannot be at all precisely stated, but the total of fresh silver used in the entire world is covered by about £3 millions or £3½ millions per annum. On the whole it may be said that of the total average of fresh supplies of silver, one-third went for such uses, and two-thirds for money. (See Appendix, page 69.) Now nothing can be supposed to lead to a greater use of silver for other purposes than money, excepting a very considerable fall in its price. But if it fell 50 per cent., it is not likely that the use would increase commensurately with the fall. So far the fall of 20 per cent. during the last six years seems not to have increased the consumption, in spite of the supposed mathematical certainty of the simple-minded theory of " supply and demand " that it " ought " to have done so. The removal of the duty of 1s. 6d. per ounce on hall-marked plate may tend to increase it in England by a fair percentage. But when it is borne in mind that the present yield of fresh silver is more than four times as high as the consumption for this purpose of the world, and that beyond this the demonetisation of £500 millions of silver is in prospect, there is no limit to the decline of price which may take place. Indeed it is quite possible that the great decline in the value of silver which is apparently in prospect will diminish the desire to look upon it as household treasure.

A suggestion of the same character is that which says : " The further fall in the price of silver will be arrested by the cessation of silver mining." No doubt certain poor silver ores and delicate processes of refining will no longer pay as well as before, but the greater quantity of silver is derived from rich ores, or in conjunction with gold. Apart, then, from possible improvements which may diminish the cost of production, this contingency will not be so effective for checking the supply as is imagined, and that the reliance on it is weak in principle and fact will be easily perceived.

The decline in the value of silver, as indicated, so far involves :—

Firstly, the worth of plate and ornaments. In 1870 it was estimated that one third of the silver in the world consisted of such, and that about one-sixth was hoarded, principally in the East. This would indicate a total amount of silver treasure in existence of say £600 millions, besides the £650 in money in 1870. Some authorities, on the supposition that much larger quantities were left before the discovery of America than is supposed (See Appendix, page 69), place the total of plate and household treasure, and objects of art, even as high as £1,000 millions. But whatever be the amount existing, apart from the quantity in use as money, the decline in the value of these treasures would not be so overwhelming a misfortune as many people, to whom this consideration may first occur, will think. It would be regretable enough, as other losses are. But for the general purposes of trade they would, like the destruction of a certain security now held in possession, only be a serious financial loss to be borne for once and done with.

In the second place the demonetisation of silver would destroy its value as currency. Assuming, on the statements before submitted, that the sum to be thus discarded be any portion of the £500 millions, the loss thereon would be great, and very distressing to the persons or States holding such silver. But it, also, would be a financial loss to be borne once for all. It does not follow that therefore these losses are to be treated lightly, for they involve a large number of millions, and this must have a most serious influence upon the wealth of individuals and on many immediate financial arrangements.

But *another point lies far beyond this.* So far the case can be likened to a person having tossed a £1 into the sea, or dropped it somewhere past recovery ; that means a loss for the individual of £1 only. But what of the thousands of people who could have made use of this piece after him, in daily circulation, in internal intercourse, as a factor with others in international trade for a thousand years or more ? Those who are free from the vulgar prejudice against money, so often expressed by poets and would-be social reformers, who are able to recognise the true dignity involved in the use of the precious metals by mankind, may therefore appreciate the main question, to which the reader has now been led up through the previous parts of this treatise.

CHAPTER VII.

The Main Question.—The Loss to the World of the Stock of Legal Tender Silver Money for the current purpose of Commerce.—The Demonetisation of Silver not a matter of choice, but of necessity.—What will be the Real Effect on Trade and Prosperity ?

The main question then is : *what would be the effect on commerce and all the social relations connected therewith, were the stock of metallic money, now amounting to say £1,400 millions, reduced by £500 millions, to £900 millions ?*

The question is put in this extreme form because, as explained before, the demonetisation of silver means the enforced adoption of the monometallic gold valuation. Whether this can be done at all, and what consequences the mere partial action taken by some nations has already brought about, is another matter. But in the chapter on the difference between full legal tender money and subsidiary coinage, it has been expressly pointed out that under the gold valuation the proportion of the latter cannot exceed a certain strictly limited amount. As stated, in England it amounts to about £16½ millions, or 10 shillings per head of population. In other gold valuing countries (Germany) this proportion has also been adopted as a guide. Indeed, under the gold systems, the demand does *not seem* to require more ; *not because there may not be a demand*, but because it is not allowed to express and develop itself properly. Without referring to the expediency and justice of these restrictions (See Appendix page 59), the fact must be noted that they forcibly limit the use of subsidiary silver coin, and in England, where prices are highest, the limitation is about 12½ per cent. of the gold circulation. Consequently, if the gold valuation becomes universal, the world—alongside of the £750 millions of gold in the world—could use only about £112 millions of such silver. If this amount, nevertheless, be taken at £150 millions it will represent the fullest possible allowance. The proportion of 12½ per cent. in England, is that of the wealthiest state, where prices are highest. In other countries, where they are lower, as in India for instance, a *larger number* of pieces will be required, but of *smaller denominations*, so that the proportion borne by their aggregate value to that of the legal tender money may be even less than it is here. It is, therefore, useless to suggest that other nations should use more token coin. Some of our economists have, for instance, even proposed that the whole of the Indian rupee coins of £200 millions should be converted into tokens, whereas the most liberal allowance for the possible use of subsidiary coins for that colony would be £30 millions. In any case the *cardinal principle of the monometallic gold system* is this *limitation of silver*. The gold valuation is not attained, until this is done as in England, and the Germans must follow the same policy. Nevertheless, although England was the first nation to demonetise silver, yet it was not until Germany joined her, in 1872, *that the evil of demonetisation became effective.*

"But," it will be asked, "why should other nations follow the example of Germany? Why should they also demonetise their silver to their own damage?" The fact is, *they cannot help themselves;* it is impossible that they can maintain a medium of exchange, which is being repudiated by other countries, and thus loses its value in international trade.

On page 9 a table is given which shows the basis upon which the equilibrium existed in 1870. Since then Germany has left the silver valuation group, and has joined the gold valuation group. She obtained £200 millions war indemnity from France, and could therefore easily accomplish her purpose of exchanging her stock of silver for gold, and she is the only country which has done so really. Without considering her losses on sales, she has thus far disposed of two-thirds of her stock. She was the first in the field, and had at least the Indian market for the sale of her silver. The stock of gold she has acquired is partly taken from France and partly from new supplies, which became subject to German control through the £200 millions of war indemnity. Of the silver discharged from Germany, a sum of about £35 millions consisted of miscellaneous French, Dutch and other silver coins which have been sent back to their original states. Of her own silver coinage the greater part has gone to India.

Germany carries with her the silver group of which she was the head. Denmark,

Sweden, and Norway have since followed in adopting gold, but they possessed little silver, and a moderate share of gold may satisfy them, besides which they are as yet far from having completed the change effectively. Holland has been so far unable to sell much silver, and has adopted a kind of bi-metallism ; but has ceased to coin silver.

The bi-metallic group of States have not only found that a large quantity of their old silver coin is being returned to them, but they have been obliged to suspend the coinage of 5 franc pieces, for obvious reasons. If the Germans and others could import their silver to France as bars, and take away the French gold at the mintage rates, France would speedily be deprived of the latter. Indeed it will be easily perceived, that France is compelled to stop the coinage of silver, because if it did not our Indian Government would soon take it into its head to export its silver to France, and congratulate itself at having thus got out of the difficulties connected with the Indian exchange. Other countries would like to make use of France in a similar way ; her action then of suspending the coinage of silver is imposed upon her, and unless the metal should be remonetised, she is only biding her time to sell her present large stock. (See Appendix, page 96.)

States under paper valuations are compelled to follow the course dictated by the leading nations. They cannot take silver because it is " cheap," for that would merely give them one depreciated currency instead of another, and if they have the power to acquire bullion at all, they must choose gold. *Only* in the event of the remonetisation of silver can this metal be of any use to them.

In the United States a kind of bi-metallism is now being attempted. Unsupported by other nations, exposed to the play of hostile action on the part of competitors, this attempt will turn out a failure. Moreover, the silver dollar of 412.5 grains deliberately debases the value of silver by 3 per cent. below the bi-metallic proportion, so that America is even in conflict with France and other states who might otherwise do their best by united action to uphold silver.

The opinion is frequently expressed, that as soon as the Germans have sold, or cease to sell, silver, the price will again rise to its previous level. This is a great error, for in the first instance the American dollar puts this out of the question, and in the second place, as soon as the Germans have done, the Latin Union, Holland and other States will sell at such fair prices as can be obtained, and these prices must necessarily be below the bi-metallic price. That the cessation of German sales and American imports of silver will have their influence on the immediate market rates, is evident, but the ups and downs likely to occur on that account will not permanently arrest the operation of the main cause of the decline. Nor is the point here involved that of the mere price of silver, whether the metal is quoted at 40 or 50, or 55 pence ; the fact that it *cannot in future serve as an international medium* of *exchange*, for the settlement of balances, as hitherto it has done *since trade began*, is the *principal point here under consideration*.

Now if the Germans have so far disposed of say £40 millions of their own silver, and the other silver and bi-metallic nations are biding their time to dispose of an aggregate of at least £150 millions more, not by their own choice, but on account of a more or less pressing necessity, it can easily be seen that the previous equilibrium is on the point of being *entirely* destroyed.

The Indian group alone remains open for the use of silver. Assuming even that the surplus stock of the other nations did not exist, that the fresh supplies from mines were half, or even less, than what they are now, India cannot take more silver than what its balance of trade warrants. Everything beyond this must enhance the prices of her produce, and thus her own currency must depreciate continually, as it is now doing. Apart from this consideration, it is scarcely possible that India and Europe could carry on an effective trade on diametrically opposed systems. The climax of the situation would arise, should India be compelled to remit money to us, as in the natural course of trade she must do at some time or another, and at the present time the aspect in this direction is already threatening. (See Appendix, page 65.) Finally, as those acquainted with the subject are already aware, our own and the Indian Government are puzzling their brains to find a means of introducing gold into India and getting rid of its silver. They cannot expect to succeed in this, but whatever violent or illusory scheme may be adopted in preference to the only practicable one, that of re-monetisation, the state of matters is clearly that silver is now driven back to its last stronghold, which has already been seriously weakened, and can hardly hold out much longer unless thus relieved. (See Appendix, page 67).

If therefore, with regard to the reduction of the metallic currency of the world, a sum of £500 millions of silver is spoken of, there is nothing extravagant in the assumption that so much as this is in jeopardy. But whether the amount to be further demonetised be only £100 or £200 millions, or less or more, the principle of the decline which it will produce on the world's trade remains the same. Considering what the effect of the only partial demonetisation by Germany has already been, the further result of the process will *almost suggest itself.*

CHAPTER VIII.

The Practical Proof of the Great Advance made in Commerce through the Increase of Metallic Money between 1848 and 1872.—The True " Theory " involved.—The Reverse Tendency caused through the Demonetisation by Human Law.

The supply of the precious metals has at all times had a marked influence on the commerce and prosperity of the world. This is not only in accordance with a natural idea, but it is borne out by the statistics available. Wars and other events have interfered now and then with progress, but the general advance was influenced by the rate of increase or decrease in the supply of gold and silver. Thus, reckoning from 1815, the prosperity of the world and of England made uninterrupted progress until 1872. Occasional " commercial crises " occurred, but they lasted only a few weeks or months. In the year following them the amount of trade increased again. From 1872, however, the trade of the world has steadily decreased, and the contraction of the metallic currency by legislation is the cause.

Some years before 1834 complaints were heard that the supply of the precious metals was scarcely adequate to the consumption in arts and for money, that in 1830 the total stock had even declined; but from 1835 to 1848 the production revived so as to satisfy at all events the then current trade. Commencing with 1836 the following table shows the exports of the produce of the United Kingdom. For the sake of simplicity the export of foreign goods from, and the importation into England need not be given, our own exports being the fair test for what concerns us here chiefly.

TABLE SHOWING THE EXPORTS OF THE PRODUCE OF THE UNITED KINGDOM FROM 1836 TO 1878, DIVIDED INTO THE PERIODS AS INDICATED.

Years.	Exports of British produce (millions).		Remarks on the stock and the supply of metallic money.
1836	£53,		*Before the discovery of the Californian and Australian gold mines.*
1837	42,	*crisis.*	
1838	50,		During this period the average annual production of gold was £6 millions, that of silver £5½ millions, together £11½ millions, of which £8 millions became monetised. The total stock of metallic money in 1848 consisted of £400 millions gold and £600 millions silver, making together say : £1,000 millions.
1839	53,		
1840	51,		
1841	52,		
1842	47,		
1843	52,		
1844	59,		
1845	60,		
1846	58,		
1847	59,	*crisis.*	
1848	53,		
1849	64,	*Californian gold mines opened.*	*From the discovery of the Californian and Australian mines to 1870.*
1850	71,		
1851	74,		
1852	78,	*Australian gold mines opened.*	
1853	99,		During this period the Californian (1849) and the Australian (1852) gold mines were opened. The average annual supply of gold rose to £22 millions, ranging from £32 millions in 1858 to £20 millions in 1870. Of the total production of gold of £490 millions, from 1849 to 1870 £350 millions, had become money. The average annual production of silver was £9 millions, ranging from, in 1849, £6 millions, 1854 £8 millions, 1868 £10 millions. Of the total of £190 millions produced in the period up to 1870 about £60 millions went into money, as has been explained before. The total stock of metallic money increased by 40 per cent., and in 1870 amounted to— £1,400 millions.
1854	97,		
1855	96,		
1856	116,		
1857	122,	*crisis.*	
1858	117,		
1859	130,		
1860	136,		
1861	125,		
1862	123,		
1863	146,		
1864	160,		
1865	166,		
1866	189,	*crisis.*	
1867	181,		
1868	179,		
1869	190,		
1870	200,		
1871	223,	*more silver produced.*	The production during the two years 1871-2 was, of gold £39 millions, and £25 millions of silver.
1872	256,		
1873	255,	*Demonetisation of silver commenced.*	*The period since the demonetisation of silver commenced.*
1874	240,		
1875	223,		
1876	201,		The yield of gold was £115 millions, having fallen to about 18 millions in 1878, the production of silver was £90 millions. the maximum being £18 millions, in 1876, the average being 15 millions. In 1878 and 1879 the production seems to have become less.
1877	199,		
1878	193,		
1879*	182,		

* Estimated on the first five months.

C

This Table first serves to show that the so-called "cycle" or crisis theory has nothing to do with the depression of trade since 1873. The years of crisis are noted, and it will be seen that the decline following was not only moderate, but was recovered shortly after, and followed up by still greater increase. But since 1873 the decline has been continuous, and no specific crisis has taken place. The allegation then, that the present bad times are only due to a "cycle," to which we are accustomed, is but one of the weak subterfuges to which the gold party has recourse.

The Table demonstrates clearly that the increase in metallic money from 1848 to 1870 of 40 per cent. was accompanied by an increase of 300 per cent. in commerce; and in 1872 the increase in British exports exceeded that of 1848 by 400 per cent. Whatever share inventions and free trade may have had in this increase, it is evident that the copious supply of metallic money afforded the medium for development in the greater measure. From this point of view metallic money seems to have a far more influential factorship than that usually assigned to it as a mere substance for "standard." As the fresh metal was monetised, so did it claim incorporation with the rest by purchases of commodities. The demand for goods increased, and prices rose, production flourished in succession; and although the holders of "fixed" incomes at first complained, yet as the production advanced prices fell again. The net result seems to be that we have had a three and four-fold production and consumption. This means "more civilisation," for amongst commodities, objects of art and books take a place as well as food for the body, and require to be fostered by the same joint agency. And thus all countries, not England alone, have benefited by a three-fold increase, and even in a greater proportion.

On the other hand, the figures since 1873 exhibit the reversal of this beneficial force through the demonetisation of silver. So far, Germany only has made a real change, affecting a sum of about £60 millions, the rest of the £500 millions remains in abeyance. So far also, the exports of England have declined from 1872 to 1878 by 24·6 per cent. It can, therefore, be left to reflection how rapidly this reverse tendency may continue. All other countries suffer more or less in the same way as England does. The present signs are all the more impressive, when it is borne in mind, that, whereas the beneficent effects of the gold discoveries thus enhanced prices and commerce, and led to an enormous increase of contracts in state loans, mercantile and industrial enterprises, and all sorts of obligations by way of natural and positive increase, the present position involves an enforced negative effect, the destructive retrospective evil of which will far outbalance the benefits previously gained.

CHAPTER IX.

The Further Loss to the World of the Annual Supplies of Silver which have hitherto nourished Internal and International Commerce.—The Insufficiency of Future Supplies of Gold.—Vain Suggestions as to Substitutes.—A Final Consideration as to the use of Subsidiary Silver Coin.

The threatening prospect of the *demonetisation of a part or the whole of the £500 millions* of money in silver is not the only evil. It concerns only the diminution in the present stock of metallic money, but, in addition to this, it must now be borne in mind, *that the future supplies of silver will also be lost to the world.* From time immemorial the annual supplies of gold *and* silver have stimulated and nourished commerce. Before 1848 the production of silver exceeded that of gold ; since 1848 gold began to predominate largely, until within the last 9 years silver increased and gold fell off, the joint total annual production during these years varied from £32 millions to £39 millions. It is stated that the present yield of gold has now fallen to £18 millions per annum, whilst that of silver has risen to £16 millions (See Appendix, pages 71 and 72). Instead of having its customary supply of the former amount as still available through the increase in silver, the world will in future have only the lessening yield of gold available for monetary purposes. The discovery of new gold fields, so often talked of, is most problematical. California and Australia were "new" countries, and their climates enabled European races to work the mines. In other tropical and foreign lands more gold may be hidden ; but the exploring zeal excited by the search for gold has not yet discovered new deposits of any note, apart from the question whether they can be worked. Indeed, the discovery of the Californian mines was an event in history, of the like of which, as regards quantity in a short time, there is no record in ancient times. It far exceeded the silver and gold discoveries in the 16th and 17th centuries. The almost simultaneous opening of the Australian mines and those of New Zealand and British Columbia rendered this event still more extraordinary. Although the public mind may now and then be excited by discoveries of gold in New Guinea, or elsewhere, there is no likelihood that such a great historical occurrence will ever happen again. The reliance upon such an indefinite prospect as the discovery of new gold fields is of a weak nature, the more so when it is borne in mind that the production of gold in the countries now yielding it, must necessarily decline, as indeed it is doing. The consumption in arts and jewelry is more or less regular, whilst the prospect of the production, or the maintenance of the present stock of gold, becomes precarious. Before long it may even be much below the proportionate increase of the population itself. If, therefore, the enforced diminution of the stock of money has already had the effect indicated, this contingency of the future repudiation of the supplies of silver aggravates the case in a still greater measure.

Many people who hear of this demonetisation of silver, suggest that the fresh supplies of gold should be used by the silver states, that the new gold found should fill up the gap. A greater misapprehension cannot be conceived. The supplies of gold have hitherto nourished the gold systems, therefore, if they are diverted from their accustomed channel, the gold States must suffer. But the suggestion is all the more absurd, if it is borne in mind that the silver States have nothing to give in exchange for gold except silver, for the "merchandise" account lies in the balance of trade. *All present contracts are based on the stock of gold and silver now in the world, and on the coming in of the annual supplies of both metals together.* Such "contracts" comprise not only all transactions in international and internal commerce now current, but those which follow thereon. The term contract does not only apply to trade, but to every arrangement in social life, in which money value plays a part—from the land owning interest to that of the humblest dependant.

The homely nursery rhyme : "Jack Spratt would eat no fat, his wife would eat no lean, nevertheless between the two, they ate the platter clean," applies in this case. As the supply of fat and lean together is absorbed by the two monetary systems, the

C 2

platter being clean, it follows that if Jack turns to fat in future, the lean becomes useless, the two must wrangle over the fat, neither of them obtaining the accustomed or necessary amount of nourishment. Let the force of this simile be enhanced by reference to the stock of fat or lean already disposed of, and its bearing upon the subject will be more appropriate still. Per contra, if Jack and his wife were to agree in future both to eat their respective shares of fat and lean, they would be very happy and prosperous.

Other suggestions are made, with a view to replenishing the vacuum. One of the readiest is: "that more bank notes should be used." Another is that "more cheques and clearing systems" should be made available. The use of bank notes rests on distinct principles, and their good or evil is principally dependant on the amount of real cash which serves for their security. The development of the banking system is sufficiently advanced, here, and even in other countries, as far as circumstances will allow. The little improvement that might be made is not only not equal to the occasion, but it would take a long time to bring about whatever it might be. On general grounds, also, it must be evident, that if cheques and clearing systems, or bank notes, have the power to replenish such a vacuum, and are therefore equivalent to solid metallic money, there is no reason why they should not be used more extensively *now*, or at *any* time, for the benefit of the world.

It is expedient now that another contingency connected with the demonetisation of silver should be pointed out. The prospect of a further fall in silver leads to the question adverted to in Chapter II., whether silver change, under its restricted tender, can be maintained in circulation at a value artificially raised above the real value of silver bullion. Thus, as long as silver bullion in England stood at 60d. per oz., our silver coin, under the restriction, could circulate at a nominal value of 66d. per oz. (See Appendix, page 59.) If, however, silver fell further, say to 45d. or lower, the questions arising are, firstly: whether the coins could continue to circulate at a value so much above their real one, and, secondly: whether other coiners besides the Mint could not manufacture silver coin of the same quality at a large profit, without the risk of being detected. There is no difficulty about such manufacture. Steel dies can be carried in the waistcoat pocket, to be used between anvil and hammer, on discs of standard silver, and the quality of the metal is the only test for good coin. It is only right that this danger should here be explicitly stated, so as to show the real nature of metallic coinage. There is, then, the prospect of the abandonment of silver for all monetary purposes, for the proposal relative to "progressively increasing the size of the subsidiary silver coin" is quite unworthy of notice.

Now if the dangers in prospect, in their first stage of development, involve,—

Firstly: the loss to the world of part or the whole of £500 millions of metallic currency, reducing the stock of 1870 from £1,400 millions to £900 millions;

Secondly: the loss of the annual supplies of silver to the trade of the world, reducing the usual annual joint yield of bullion from say £34 millions to £18 millions;

Thirdly: the possible abandonment of the token silver coinage of say £150 millions, reducing the stock of money further by that amount;—

it is certainly time that the public should be warned against the consequences.

What are wars, revolutions, and other serious events in their effects upon commerce and society in comparison to what is here in prospect? Even if the matter of demonetisation does not go farther than it has now gone, and the consequences be allowed to develop themselves, the state of things demands immediate attention. The changes which must follow in international trade, in the monetary economy of individual countries, and in other matters connected therewith, may bring about rapid modifications in the prosperity of nations, of which a near future will give us examples which we may be too late to profit by. They may cause a redistribution of property, and may possibly entail social upheavings of which the uneasy movements at present perceptible are the mere obscure preliminary symptoms.

CHAPTER X.

England's Interest in this matter.—Her Stock of Gold is not the Greatest.—Table indicating the Present Division of Metallic Money.—The British Empire the largest holder of Silver.—England may be ultimately drained of Gold.

But what are England's interests in this matter? In the above portion of this treatise the " general " interests of the world have been spoken of. It is not unlikely that many persons, hearing that England has had a gold currency for more than 60 years, will think " England is therefore in a safe position, and has done wisely." Further, on the old assumption that when one loses, the other must gain, they may think that " England must here be the gainer." Others may, however, have at once perceived that England's interests are bound up with the prosperity of the rest of the world more than any other nation, and may also know that there are certain cases which bring loss to *all* parties *alike*.

England has a far greater stake in this question of silver, because, in the first place, the British Empire is the largest holder of silver. From the statements in Chapters IV. and V. this might be inferred, but as since 1870 several changes have taken place, it is expedient that the situation at the end of 1878 should here be indicated. Since Germany demonetised silver she has acquired a stock of gold which, with the bullion in the imperial bank, is now about £100 millions. She has £19 millions of silver yet for sale. France and the Latin Union have received back a great many silver 5 franc pieces circulating elsewhere. Silver has returned to Holland, but the Dutch have acquired some gold. The Scandinavian States have obtained a moderate quantity of gold. The United States have increased their stock of gold and coined some silver. From 1870 to 1878 the exports of silver to the East, at the reduced value, amount to £56 millions. The production of gold during that time was £134 millions, that of silver £97 millions. Making allowance for the portion of this fresh accession used for other purposes (somewhat less than before), £110 millions of gold and £70 millions of silver have been added to the general stock of hard money in the world. So there are now

In 1878 Gold   £850 millions.
,,   Silver ...   £720 ,,

The following table shows how this may now be divided in 1878. It is made up from the best information as to what share of silver has since been added to subsidiary and fractional coinage. But as the statistics of general coinage in recent years are not yet fully available, until certain allowances have been made for the remaining bullion bars, the statement must be taken as approximate.

TABLE SHOWING THE PROBABLE DISTRIBUTION OF THE PRESENT STOCK OF GOLD AND SILVER MONEY IN 1878 (IN MILLIONS STERLING).

	LEGAL TENDER MONEY.		SUBSIDIARY.
	Gold.	Silver.	Silver coin.
British Empire.			
United Kingdom	£135	—	£18
British Colonies, with India, &c.	45	300	7
Continental Europe.			
France and Latin Union	310	130	11
Germany	100	19	20
Other States	70	30	9
America.			
United States, Mexico, Central and South America	45	40	24
Other States.			
China, Japan, &c., and not accounted for ...	145	112	—
	£850	£631	£89

It will thus be seen that the British Empire holds nearly one-half of the silver money in the world, apart from the fact that England is rich in silver plate, and that India is supposed to possess in bangles and hoarded silver an amount about equal to that in money. The Indian rupee coinage, together with bar silver, cannot now be less than £250 millions. In China there is probably a far greater amount than here stated, principally hoarded; and considering that so many Eastern and other countries are under the influence of the English trade, it is not too much to assume that the greater portion of silver is owned by British subjects.

Of other nations, France holds the greater portion now, her stock of 5-franc pieces may have increased by £40 millions since 1870. But she has also regained her former stock of gold, and the balance of trade is generally so much in her favour that she is accumulating more. A State like France, which can pay away £200 millions for war indemnity in three years, and so soon recover itself, can also bear the loss on the demonetisation of her silver, if need be. She would be able to take gold from England to make up the gap. Other nations than France, less rich in gold, will be driven to do the like. If the stock of both metals were fairly divided all over the world, the demonetisation of silver would be as serious, but trade might, nevertheless, go on in a less disturbed manner.

Under the actual situation, however, the world being divided into gold States on the one hand, *versus* bi-metallic and silver States on the other, in the manner shown, the two latter are forced, by whatever means there are available, to obtain gold. It will be admitted that they cannot sell their silver, because all want to, and are forced to sell. The only remedy they have is to strive to import less, and to export more goods, so as to prevent money leaving the country, and to acquire the power of obtaining gold. That they first recur to the policy of protection is easily understood. That, secondly, they cannot pay us in silver, is only an additional force compelling them to abstain from buying our goods. And rich as England is, much as gold now accumulates at the Bank of England, for want of employment, it will find its speedy outlet as soon as the other nations have crept up to the position necessary for that purpose. Foreign nations, including France, thus hedge themselves in; England's policy has been the true one of free trade, and if she now lies open to all the world, the danger threatening free trade originates solely in the " demonetisation " of silver.

The fact then that England now has a gold currency of £135 millions is in itself no important advantage to her. Her export trade has already fallen off by an amount much exceeding the entire sum of £135 millions (See Appendix, page 53). Her purchasing power, whether for goods or currency, whether through lesser quantity or lower prices, has already greatly declined, and it is not at all impossible that under all the circumstances, England and India will be stranded together upon the silver basis itself.

CHAPTER XI.

More than Three-quarters of the Commerce of England with Other nations rested on the Silver Basis.—Our trade on the Gold basis has increased.—The Decline is in the trade on the Silver basis.—The Fall in the Price of Silver acts more injuriously than a High Protective Tariff.—The Plain Cause of the Decline.

The fact that the British Empire is the largest holder of silver is exceeded by a much more important consideration :

England has also the greatest interests in silver, because more than three-fourths of the whole of her outward commerce is conducted on the silver basis, one-fourth only resting on gold. Accordingly the trade of this country with gold States ought not to have decreased, whilst that on silver must have declined. *That is precisely the case.* In the Appendix, page 47, a full statement of our exports to all countries is given with the explanations requisite respecting their systems of valuation, to which reference may be made for showing the following general result :

EXPORTS OF THE PRODUCE OF THE UNITED KINGDOM.

From the Year 1874 to 1878,

Increase on British export on the *gold interest*
£53,374,000 to £56,812,000 ...   ...   or   6.4 per cent.
Decrease of British exports on the *silver interest*
£184,852,000 to £135,992,000   ...   .   or   26.4   ,,

But if the trade with the same States as grouped in the Table on page 48 is taken at its aggregate in 1872, we have

From 1872 to 1878,

Increase on British exports on the *gold interest*
£52,068,000 to £56,812,000 ...   ...   or   9.1   ,,
Decrease on British exports on the *silver interest*
£203,893,000 to £133,992,000   ...   .   or   33.3   ,,

The fact is that the countries with whom we trade in gold alone, by way of effective metallic exchange, are the Australian colonies, New Zealand, and British Columbia as being our own gold fields. The greater part of their yield has gone to France and the Latin Union. In spite of bad trade, then, our exports to Australia have increased as usual. This is not the consequence of emigration, for the decline in prices exceeds this by far. Moreover, our trade with France, and other countries where increase of population plays no such part, has increased, because gold is available. In all cases where the gold basis is not real, or in bi-metallic States where silver begins to predominate, the decline is marked, whilst the trade with the silver States of 1872 has fallen off without an exception.

Since 1872 our exports to Germany have declined by 35 per cent. That a country which has received £200 millions of money in three years should purchase so much less seems surprising, but the reason is perfectly obvious. Germany's export trade suffers in as great a measure as our own, her industry is at a low ebb. If she imported more goods she would be unable to keep her newly-acquired gold; her statesmen, therefore, propose " protection." Holland, Sweden, Norway, and Denmark, who are trying to establish a gold valuation, show a still more serious falling off in the purchase of our goods. As regards all other countries who have not as yet taken any similar steps, for the simple reason that they have no power whatever to help themselves, the decline of trade with us *is still more certain.*

Silver arrived here in payment to us. from one country, and was available for payments from us to another in full value. Since the demonetisation set in, this facility threatens to come to an end. The stock of silver in the world has hitherto served for the purposes of international exchanges in the same way as gold. England was one of the countries exchanging most silver, although she had chosen gold for her internal use. Besides the usual dealings in the stock there were the fresh supplies from mines coming to the London market, stimulating England's trade in all directions. Other European or manufacturing nations have but a secondary interest in this, not only because their international trade is not so extensive, but because the commercial position and policy of this country enables them to make use of it as an intermediary, so to speak, in matters of exchange.

The reason why silver dealing States can no longer import as freely as before will easily be seen. British goods cannot be sold to them unless at an advance of, at present, about 30 per cent. on previous prices, and the uncertainty of the value of silver makes this charge a more serious preventive to trade than a deliberately high tariff. They therefore hardly need " protection," were it not for the purpose of guarding the enforced home industry necessary to furnish them with substitutes, such as they may be. Naturally also, if they imported and. actually paid for more goods, they would lose more currency when the balance of trade is against them. A corresponding rise in the value of their exports would not compensate them, but confirm the deterioration of their metallic money. This is the case in several silver States where both import and export have fallen off.

As regards paper using States, the prospect of their recovering specie payments since Demonetisation made silver useless as an international means of exchange, is all the more remote. Their exchanges are consequently so precarious, that they actually cannot import and *pay for* British goods, without causing an immediate rise in the rates of Exchange, which places imported goods at a disadvantage to the inferior home manufactures. States can be named, now labouring under a depreciation on their notes, where, if they imported, *and paid for*, half a milllion sterling of English goods, the exchange would rise by 10 or more per cent. at once. Italy, for instance, is a case in point, the " margin " thus created by the delicacy of her Exchange is such, that she can actually produce cotton goods woven by the hand-loom and hand-shuttle; and within the last year or two this industry has been revived. The Russian home industry flourishes for the same reason.

But it is not the mere fall in the price of silver which is the cause of trouble. Whether the price be 45 or 50 or 55 pence per ounce, the fact that silver can no longer serve the purpose of international exchanges as formerly, is the real difficulty, Silver dealing States must endeavour to uphold its value for internal use by preventing its export at low exchange, and but for this struggle between the international and current value, the price would have fallen much lower. They can prevent the export of silver only by importing less goods from countries like England. The necessity of doing this is so strong, that it not only finds expression in the respective national accounts of trade, but is forced upon merchants, who find that they cannot import as before without incurring loss.

Many of our "professors" of commercial economy know nothing whatever of the plain motives which guide trade and exchanges in this respect. All that they can do is to preach to the British public that the rules of "supply and demand" must conquer from the "British manufacturing" point of view. Foreign nations *must* take British goods, they fancy! The fact that our own importing power has so quickly declined within the last year is bitter sarcasm on so great an error.

The same authorities talk of "overproduction," unable to appreciate that in the foregoing there are causes which might be said to create "under-consumption." And those who know upon how refined a scale of profit business is based now-a-days, can, in view of the hard facts here pointed out, understand why England's trade has already fallen off so seriously. Silver has already to a considerable extent ceased to be a medium for the purchase of merchandise, and this process threatens to go still further. Now if silver were again used as legal tender money, the bar to business would be removed, and both for the silver and the paper valuing States the "cash-basis" would again become operative. Upon such cash-basis the natural competition of England's manufactures could not be resisted. International merchants and bankers are well acquainted with the absolute effects of these causes.

CHAPTER XII.

The State Debts of Nations incurred on the joint gold and silver basis.—The Difficulty of Paying Interest and Capital increased.—The Alternative of Less Import by, or Bankruptcy of Certain Nations.—Prospect of Loss to England by Repudiation of these Debts, or further Falling Off in Exports.—Inevitable Destruction of Free Trade.

The difficulties which thus compel other countries to abstain from buying goods from us are enhanced by a further consideration. Most of the nations have largely increased their States debts and other obligations during the last thirty years. These were contracted for on the basis of prices and trade as it rested on the use of both gold and silver in the world. And as this is now so greatly affected by the partial demonetisation of silver, the question arises whether interest and capital can be repaid. Both the creditor and the debtor States will suffer in consequence.

The State debts of the nations are as follows :—

Nations.					Debts.		
England					£785 millions.		⎫
France					750	„	⎪
Germany					165	„	⎬ Held by the nations themselves.
Holland					80	„	⎪
Belgium					36	„	⎪
Denmark					14	„	⎪
					——		⎭ £1,830 millions.
United States	...	...	...	...	£400 millions.		⎫
Russia	...	...	...	...	375	„	⎪
Austria-Hungary	...	...	...	...	346	„	⎪
Italy ...	...	. .	...	...	251	„	⎪
Spain	...	...	...	...	260	„	⎪
Turkey	...	...	...	...	215	„	⎬ Held to the greater extent by other nations.
India ...	...	...	...	...	106	„	⎪
Egypt	...	...	...	...	95	„	⎪
Mexico	...	...	...	...	79	„	⎪
Brazils	...	...	...	...	68	„	⎪
Portugal	...	...	...	...	66	„	⎪
British Colonies	...	...	...	...	63	„	⎪
South American and other small States	...				295	„	⎭ £2,619 millions.
							£4,449 millions.

The-first named six nations not only keep their own debts as investments at home, and are therefore not obliged to send money abroad for payment of interest or capital, but they also hold a portion of the State debts of the other nations, and *receive money* on that account. They may be called "internationally wealthy" nations. The others do not own any foreign loans, but a great portion of their debts is held by the wealthy countries. Assuming that out of the total of £2,670 millions owing by the internationally "indebted" nations, £2,000 millions are held elsewhere, and stating their value as amounting to £1,700 millions, it appears that

England	-	holds £750 millions,
France	-	„ £450 „
Germany	-	„ £400 „
Holland ⎫		
Switzerland ⎬	hold £100 „
Belgium ⎭		

Adding other claims in railway stocks, industrial enterprises, in shipping, and other investments abroad to this share in international debts,

England has a total *outward wealth of* from £1,000 *to* £1,050 *millions.*

The great distinction between the wealth of States like England, France, &c., compared to that of the internationally indebted countries, lies in this fact. In every country there are lands, houses, enterprises, household goods, and other home possessions. Whether they are more or less in quantity or quality, or of higher or lower local value, does not much matter, but it is obvious that the general claim of State and other indebtedness makes the really important difference in wealth. England's great advantage, therefore, is that she holds the largest amount of such "international" claims. The income which England derives from this outward property is between £55 to £60 millions per annum, and she has consequently been able to import more goods than she exported. The fact is, that England is in the position of a manufacturer as well as capitalist. Nevertheless, it must not bo assumed that this advantage is unlimited, for the figures involved are fairly before us, and the amounts lost in defaults, and the falling off in exports are already considerable (See Appendix, page 53).

If, then, a portion of England's purchasing power rests on these claims, it is easy to see how precarious the situation becomes as regards many of these foreign State loans, which have been incurred on the scale of prices established during the period of 1850 to 1872, viz.: on the *full stock of gold and silver*, and kept up *by the yearly supply of* both. Our own Stock Exchange and foreign Bourses granted them on the representations of accounts formed thereon. Through the present decline in prices, it is obvious that the payment of interest (not to speak of the redemption of capital) becomes all the more difficult. The *first and most favourable alternative* which then presents itself is this: if these foreign nations continue honestly to discharge their obligations in state debts to us, *they cannot buy so much, they have less to spare for British goods.*

Further, a large portion of these loans have been employed in reproductive works, calculated to increase the quantities of the exports from these states, which they anticipated they would be able to dispose of here. The fall in prices has not only reduced the profits on their exports, but as they can only import a smaller proportion of our manufactures, our power of consumption is diminished. As soon as the ball is thus set rolling, a period of ever increasing reaction sets in, to the permanent restriction of international trade. The inability of the foreign debtor states to pay will then be followed by each .nation being self-contained, and the whole system of international trade must be commenced *de· novo*, on a fresh basis. This involves the *second alternative*, the *bankruptcy*, wholly or in part, of the *debtor nations.*

It may thus happen that, although the holders of so-called fixed income derived from these sources will benefit through lower prices, yet through this very cause the fixed income itself will be destroyed. But, if the previous progress of trade had not been interrupted by the demonetisation of silver, these States would be able to discharge their debts. If the present enhanced supplies of silver were available for the further nourishment and increase of the prosperity of commerce, these debts could have been liquidated with facility. Under the present circumstances the affairs of these and other nations fall under the sway of a mathematical necessity, against which it is idle to protest. All the multifarious and interwoven interests including State matters, public undertakings, mercantile and private contracts, and all other social obligations are herein involved, and compel the statesmen of each country to guard its interests.

If we in England then object to foreign countries recurring to protection, let us recollect one thing. The success of the free trade movement, initiated by England, can to a great extent be ascribed to the great and rapid advance which commerce made during the period of the gold discoveries. It was contemporary with those discoveries, and the sweeping benefits brought about by the ample supplies of money overcame certain distinctions in the economical positions of nations. And free trade would have been continually fostered but for the harsh and restrictive agency of deliberate legislation now at work. The demonetisation of silver now gives an importance to these differences of position, which becomes paramount. As yet the decline of trade is not due to the actual extension of protection abroad, but is solely owing to the demonetisation of silver. The interests of England beyond this, concern the doubt as to the ability of certain foreign nations to pay the debts due, and the necessity all nations are under of importing still less from us so as to be able to discharge them, as far as they may.

CHAPTER XIII.

Foreign Competition is not the Cause of Decline in our Trade.—Other Nations complain of our Competition.—Injustice of Certain Allegations.—The Real Cause may now force other Nations to Manufacture for themselves.—England's Natural Right to be the Principal Manufacturer, and the Foundation of her present Position.

Foreign competition has not caused the decline in our trade. Our exports had continually increased up to 1872, and the suggestion that foreign nations should at once have made such an improvement in their manufactures so as to lead to the rapid decline in ours in a year or two is preposterous, even in theory. That other manufacturing nations have not taken our trade away is shown by the fact that they all, like ourselves, loudly complain of loss of export and dullness in the home trade, and attribute the cause of the former to England's competition. The depression extends to all kinds of industry, for some of which we have exclusive advantages. Certain changes in the manufacturing processes of working nations will always happen; just as we have learnt from, and owe the introduction of some important branches of industry to foreigners, so will progress in inventions extend, as they have always done in all ages. But this cannot bring about a sudden change, such as is implied by the above suggestion. It may also happen that the necessities of certain countries require extraordinary efforts in economy, as was the case in England, when, after the Napoleonic wars, great and successful efforts were made to reconquer wealth by exports. Thus in recent years, the United States had to recover specie payment, by lessening their imports and encouraging their exports. Were America enabled to send us her silver in fair payment, she would import relatively more from us. Altogether if the general prosperity of the world's trade had not been so violently interrupted, if the fresh supplies of silver had been used to enhance it, the falling off of our American trade would have been more than compensated for in many other directions.

Among other allegations, that which attributes the falling off to the growing inferiority of British goods is the most untrue. No other nation can as yet outrival England in the production of suitable goods. If certain natives in the East require light cotton goods well-charged with glaze, because their cheapness is a set-off against washing, they and the British merchant know what they are about. Foreigners cannot give such or better goods at the same price. All other more or less disjointed allegations directed against our industry, of a similar nature are useless, even that which blames the British workman for his strikes. Strikes have occurred in all manufacturing countries. How far they are caused by the very question of justice involved here may ultimately appear. Whatever advance in prices strikes have caused, its proportion to the total has not been so large a percentage as to give foreigners any opportunity of profiting by it; and the reduction in prices effected since 1872, exceeds the previous advance. The charge of insobriety brought against the skilled British workman, on whom our superiority in manufacturing is really dependent, is moreover unjust. All other endeavours thus to throw blame in any direction, rather than pay attention to the matter here brought forward, are but signs of the confusion under which we are labouring in consequence.

But, although *foreign competition has not yet had* any effect at all, yet there is now *the great danger that it will soon become effective.* This does not imply that our present rivals in industry can beat us, it *means that nations which have not manufactured* for themselves *will now be forced to do so.* Whatever we may have to say to them in regard to our goods and rules of trade, their simple answer will be : " You will not take payment in our money, so we must either go without your goods, or make our own clothing and other requisites." That they will not be able at first to produce goods as suitable and valuable as our own is obvious ; but, as has been shown before, the fall in the price of silver and the delicacy of the rates of exchange, amount to an aggregate of margins which enable foreign nations to manufacture stuffs by the common old-fashioned methods. And when this kind of industry is improved by machinery, it may *permanently replace our own manufactures.* The sad part of this prospect is, that those who now refuse to recognise the main cause of our loss of trade, will then be able to lay all to the charge of this actual foreign manufacture.

In a country like this the bulk of the population is dependent on the exports of the produce of labour for the acquisition of a large portion of daily food and other matters. There is nothing artificial in this position ; it is on the contrary the natural result of free trade and of our general progress and intelligence. But if other nations, better fitted by climate and other reasons to produce articles of food and raw materials, were compelled to neglect these resources, and to take to manufacturing, there would be something artificial in such a result. It is immaterial whether one nation produces commodities in factories, the other from the soil, all that is required being the uninterrupted course of trade and exchange. From this point of view, all the talk that there are too many people in this country, and that it cannot grow sufficient food, is futile and unintelligent. It is said that the recent bad home harvests require an additional importation of £15 millions in food, which we obtain easily and cheaply from elsewhere. But what is most significant is that, although the people from whom we obtain this, thus acquire from us so much greater a power for the purchase of our goods, take rather less from us than before.

Many of the features of England's political power and internal social life originated in her comparative superiority in manufacturing, and are still entirely dependent on its maintenance. The present decline in trade already shows its effect upon the value of land and property. We already see its extension to those dependent on fixed income from loans to other countries, and finally to those dependent on home enterprises, the interest or profit on which is no longer obtainable. Our banking institutions are thrown under a cloud, and many other features of our social arrangements begin to be called into question Of the suffering which exists among the poorer classes, and which may yet become much more distressing, it is not necessary to speak. But that the state of confusion and contradiction under which so many matters are now labouring should not be left to right itself by chance will be admitted. That which has here been said as to the contraction of the currency by the demonetisation of silver, at all events keeps open a distinct issue, which would seem to show that the prospect is very unfavourable for England. The inveterate adherents to the exclusive gold system here and elsewhere may continue to scorn this issue and the facts, but the common sense of the people of this country may recognise their validity before it is too late. For, if in the opinion of many, the impression should have been created, that the cause here assigned has even *contributed* to produce this effect, its consideration is commanded by both personal interest and patriotism against all the current doctrines of its opponents.

CHAPTER XIV.

The question of India and her Valuation.—Vain suggestions.—The Council Drafts (See Appendix, page 64).—The Decline in the Import and Export Power of India.—Precarious State of her Balance of Trade and Finances.—The Remonetisation of Silver alone can rescue India.

The subject of India, with her valuation, is an integral portion of the whole case, which has here been purposely reserved. It is the great puzzle with which we have to deal, taxing the ingenuity of all sorts of schemers in vain. Some of these want to reduce the whole Indian silver coinage to the position of tokens, and others even go so far as to propose to diminish the amount of metal in the coins and keep them nevertheless at their previous current value. Some expect the Indian population to give up their jewellery and have it converted into gold coin. Other still more fanciful proposals have been made, to which it does not seem necessary to refer, because they studiously overlook the real facts of the case as they formerly stood, and as they now stand even after recent changes.

In England the losses which private people suffer on income payable in rupees, and those of the State, due to the exchange, create most attention, although those borne by merchants and bankers are far more serious. The losses incurred are due solely *to the demonetisation of silver*. This cause is mathematically certain in its nature, and nothing but the remonetisation of silver can counteract the effect produced.

It has been alleged that the council drafts made by the Home Government of India have contributed to the fall in silver, but it must be borne in mind, that in reality, these council drafts are only a different method of settling an account. (See Appendix, page 64). Under the old East India Company, the supplies sent out for military and governmental purposes were accounted for in a different way; and it may be alleged that the annual withdrawals of *employés* of the Company, and others who had made rapid fortunes in India, were very considerable. If, through increased loans and more effective government, the charges have now increased, they ought to be fairly covered by the increased prosperity of India, and with its extended commerce the country ought to be able to absorb the usual quantity of silver.

Through the demonetisation of silver, India, in common with China, is not only threatened with the demonetised stock in Europe, but with the whole of the fresh annual supplies of the mines, of which three-fifths formerly went to Europe. India cannot absorb more than a fraction of her share above the customary balance of trade, and if, through loans raised here, she has taken a few millions more in silver than she would have done, at a reduced price, she has thereby already suffered the depreciation of the whole of her silver currency of £200 millions by 15 to 20 per cent. The effects of the depreciation of silver, on both her exports and imports, are most marked. Manchester manufacturers and others complain that they cannot sell goods to India as formerly, alleging that the Indian tariff is the cause of this falling off. In reality it is the decline of silver, which raises the price of British goods in rupees by 25, or more, per cent., and decreases the consumption. And moreover :—if India were to import, say only £2 millions per annum of British goods more than she now does, the exchange would fall much lower. If India were to import, say, £5 millions more, so as to destroy the small balance of trade which still exists in her favour after deducting the council drafts, she would be reduced to remitting silver here. Such silver would be practically worthless, showing most strikingly the effect produced on the Exchange, or the "loss of the power of payment in silver." With all this, the Indian markets are overstocked with British goods ; on the other hand, our warehouses in England are overloaded with Indian commodities ; for speculation, natural on the recent movements in the price of silver, has caused undue shipments in both directions. The financial position of the Indian Government and that of the people are in a precarious state, and were it not for the loans raised here during the last few years, India would have lost the power of importing bullion altogether. Indeed, the forcible injection of silver into India is one of the worst features of the matter, for it lowers both the value of her currency and increases her indebtedness. (See Appendix, page 67).

India is, nevertheless, the largest holder of silver in the world. Some people allege that between England and India, the bi-metallic system is virtually in existence, because the one uses gold and the other silver ; the deliberate perversion involved in which allegation would best appear were India compelled to make payment in silver to us, as she may be compelled to do if she be not rescued from her present danger. It is fortunate, perhaps, for the sake of the general interest of the world, that this Indian question goes so close to the heart and the interests of England. The gigantic problem of the Indian valuation cannot be solved, or the threatened danger averted, unless silver be brought back to its previous value. The value of silver can only be restored by its remonetisation, to which England must become an active party.

Besides India, there are other British colonies under the silver valuation, which increase the obligations of this country in the same direction. Indeed, with the exception of the Australian Colonies, all other British possessions are greatly dependent on silver, and the aggregate of the interests which they involve is larger than that of India. Our Indian trade represents but one-sixth of that done on the silver basis. (See Appendix, page 49.)

CHAPTER XV.

The only Remedy.—The Remonetisation of Silver.—Germany's Motives for the Demonetisation.—Which of the Nations should Remonetise ?—An International Agreement only can bring about this Remonetisation.—England has the greatest Interest in its Success.—The International Conference in Paris of 1878 : Why it failed.—The need for another Conference.

In the preceding chapters the complete statement of the case has been brought before the reader, in order to prepare for the consideration of the plain remedy which alone can rescue England and the world from the present precarious position. *That remedy is simply* "the remonetisation of silver."

Those who have fully understood the reasons for the existence of the previous equilibrium and its recent destruction, will no doubt have already come to this plain logical conclusion. The most natural suggestion would seem to be : that Germany, being the more immediate cause of the upset, should retrace her steps, and change again from gold to silver. There are people who say that Germany had no occasion to make the change from silver to gold, because the basis of prices current there was lower than here. The difference in the price of labour between England and Germany does not warrant the allegation, and when England adopted the gold valuation in 1816 her prices were much lower than those of Germany in 1872. Germany can also say that she adopted the gold system in imitation of England, and that she now has very nearly completed it. Moreover, she has this special reason to advance : that, if she re-adopted the silver valuation or took to the bimetallic system, she would, like all the rest of the States, be liable again to the play of monometallism between the English and Indian group. She can, at all events, plead, that in the position which she has adopted, she secured herself against this invidious counterplay, and this is perhaps one of the strongest proofs that the responsibility of the whole conflict rests upon England.

France and the Latin Union States cannot do more than uphold the use of silver, for the time being, in the way they now do. With them the question is rather that of whether they must not also demonetise it, unless others agree to co-operate in its maintenance. In the United States the silver dollar has again been introduced, but it is quite evident that their bi-metallism cannot be maintained without much more effective support. In spite of a recent resolution of the American Legislature to maintain the dollar at any risk, the Americans will see this truth. They have lately become again a metallic State, and it must be distinctly understood that they have recovered this position exclusively on the gold basis, and for the present remain on that basis. Indeed, the silver coined has not only not contributed to the recovery, but at this time is rather an encumbrance to it. If the silver dollars had to be given up, the United States would certainly lose the purchasing power of several millions per annum, but this would chiefly affect England. England would lose the benefit of this power of selling more goods to America and the re-exchange of silver with other nations. The Americans, therefore, will perceive that they had better carry out their present policy of encouraging their own manufactures and the economical tendency forced upon them.

In truth the *whole matter depends upon England's willingness to join other nations* in upholding silver for the general good, and that of herself and.India primarily.

Those not acquainted with the course which has been pursued lately must now be informed that the United States invited the nations to an *International Conference* on the question, held in Paris in September, 1878. To this monetary conference called for the purpose of effecting an international agreement between nations, our Government sent delegates. It appears that these delegates were instructed not to take any prominent or leading part in the conference; that, in fact, they were strictly tied down not to depart from the system of England. If this were not known, the share which they took in the proceedings would seem to have been somewhat contradictory. Protesting, in the strongest terms, through one of the members, against the extension of the gold valuation, and against the demonetisation of silver as involving ruin and destruction to commerce, they yet proposed deliberately that no agreement should be come to, that each State or group should follow its own course. Their allegation that England had contributed nothing towards the demonetisation of silver, in face of the fact that she was the first to demonetise it in 1816, was singular enough. But when they prided themselves upon England having done nothing towards this end, because the silver valuation in·India had not been abrogated, they adopted a method of stating the case which is scarcely in accord with the real situation. For not only was England perfectly, powerless to introduce a change into India, but, excepting for the fact that India is ruled by Englishmen, that colony stands to all intents and purposes in the position of a foreign nation. Indeed, it is just the conflict between England and India, borne prior to 1872, by the bi-metallic group, which had been, and continues to be, at the bottom of all the mischief. The refusal to recognize this, or rather the manner in which the real position was thus avoided, with the view apparently of inducing other nations *to take the chestnuts out of the fire*, is a piece of " Monetary diplomacy," as Monsieur Henri Cernuschi terms it, of an extraordinary character. It had not even the merit of taking into account the question whether other nations were able to do what our British delegates wished. For not only have other nations no power to maintain silver, and the bi-metallic system, by themselves, but the maintenance of the. opposing English and Indian monometallic systems would render such ability, if they had it, utterly futile. And if, under the liberty which our English delegates reserved for each group of States, it was implied, that in the meanwhile preparations might be made for India's adoption of the gold valuation, the insinuation that other nations should not demonetise silver, or should continue on the bi-metallic system, places the matter beyond the reach of criticism. The English delegates, as stated above, however, adopted the attitude here described not from strict personal convictions, but as representing the position which this country has assumed, under what may be called its current conceptions on the gold valuation. In that case, as guarding the dignity of the English system hitherto clung to, the matter is so far explicable.

It would perhaps appear that at this Paris monetary conference, our delegates had too much confidence in the then existing state of things; that they were

D

too much influenced by the non-attendance of Germany, and by certain violent opposition made by one or two of the smaller States. In Germany, a strong party is rising against the exclusive gold valuation; its principal promoters themselves are willing to admit that universal bi-metallism is the proper remedy. Among the small States, Switzerland was represented by a delegate whose views in favour of gold are extreme. Switzerland has never coined much else than subsidiary silver, and if she should stand aloof from an international arrangement, if her common sense does not lead her to disavow her uncompromising representative, she may either be ignored, or punished through the commercial policy which other States may adopt. Similar remarks apply to other small States and captious objectors, who, in reality, have neither the theoretical nor the practical right to thwart the resolves of the leading monetary nations.

The allegation, that such international conferences are but chimeras, has been made and *can only* be made, by the implacable advocates of gold, who have brought this country to its present precarious position by studiously enforcing their theories upon other nations. At the conference in Paris our delegates were said to have attended only as a matter of courtesy to other nations, but in spite of this reserve they passed resolutions distinctly affirming disagreement. If nations can meet in conference thus to agree to disagree, they might as well agree to agree. All this lies exclusively in England's hands. If she can promulgate free trade to all nations, and enter into treaties with them, she can agree with them on this matter, and promote free trade with it. It is the duty of England, therefore, to act in this matter with a due energy, which the full appreciation of the subject demands. If she fail in this, all the consequences previously predicted, and now being verified by events, will be fulfilled.

If, on the other hand, England is willing to contribute towards the remonetisation of silver, the first practical steps towards this end will at once change the present depression of trade. The uncertain dark times will be turned into a period of speedy re-establishment, and a future brighter even than what we have hitherto witnessed in the world's prosperity will be the result. Those who are able to recognise the effects caused by the demonetisation of the silver now in use, and the loss of the future supplies, will also be ready to admit, that when this agent is rescued from its present lethargy and threatened death, when its fresh and even increased supply is again nourishing international and internal intercourse, there *will* be such a period of enhanced prosperity. The decision between great ruin and social upheavings, the nature of which we can only imagine with consternation; and, on the other hand, increased happiness and all the benefits of civilisation attendant thereon, thus hang upon a slender thread, *i.e.*, the turn which our Government and Economists may take in the matter. These are the reasons why England should take a prominent part in the promotion of another international conference, with the view of bringing about an agreement.

CHAPTER XVI.

The Prevailing Doctrine of Monometallism.—The Sacrifice demanded on its behalf. —The Doctrine false in Fact.—The Interest of the Creditor.—Other Objections to the use of Silver are of little importance as regards the Main Question.

The attitude of our delegates at the Paris Conference was necessarily influenced by the prevailing doctrine which makes many persons in England and elsewhere so persistent in favour of the gold valuation. In the Appendix (page 87) the controversy upon this point is described, but it may be useful that its main feature should be alluded to now. The common typical English economist adheres to the gold valuation, and refuses to hear anything in favour of silver—firstly, because it is *our* system, and has entailed habits which he thinks right and proper. He fails to understand that the success of our system was due to the causes herebefore elucidated—viz., the equilibrium or counterbalance between the four groups of valuation.

But above all this, our ordinary economist has faith in the saying—"*Money is the standard or measure of value, we must only have one measure or unit* of value, and the "*human*" *law cannot establish fixed proportions* between gold and silver." Accepting this as a logical maxim, it is no wonder that he disdains any other suggestion with a kind of impatient obstinacy. Nevertheless, it can be maintained that the above saying is nothing more than an almost meaningless phrase, invented by some of the old authorities for want of something better, and conveying a false impression. Money, or gold and silver, singly or combined, are just as little standards or measures of value as the air and the water. Like these they are only factors, *necessary factors*, it is true, in the system of intercourse. Alongside of other methods of exchange, banking and clearing-house systems, with which we are so well acquainted here in this country, metallic coin performs simple and distinct purposes in internal and international commerce. *The value of things*, like the definition of the pound sterling, depends upon hundreds of factors and considerations, and the currency has only a certain indirect influence, whose potentiality rests upon natural numerical proportions in a sense different from that of measure (See Chapter VIII., p. 18). Now, if this apparently strong logical conception is in reality false, it follows that the doctrine involved in the necessity for our having but one "measure," with its allusion as to the inability of the law to maintain fixed proportions between gold and silver, loses its power. The question, then, of whether the power of the human law is able to fix these proportions for the purposes of currency, alone remains. It is remarkable that this power should be denied, when, here in England, we deliberately coin silver of a lower metallic value, and supply the difference by the direct force of law. The answer that the tender of these pieces is limited to £2, does not invalidate this truth. It is evidence of the *positive* force exercised by legislation; and of its *negative* force, the present fall in the price of silver, due to the demonetisation by law, is abundant proof.

The objectors to the concurrent use of gold and silver say, amongst other things, that if both these metals were found in precisely equal quantities, there would be no objection whatever to the bi-metallic system. It is perfectly obvious that such a mathematical agreement is impossible in nature, for in the mathematical sense, it ought to agree day by day, and hour by hour. It seems singular that because such is not the case, and we choose to deny the power of the human law, and take no notice of the continued demand, that, therefore, we should say, "Let us demonetise one-half, or one entire factor of the two of which the metallic money of the world is now composed, and refuse to accept the future accustomed supply." *Doctrines demanding such fatalism and fanaticism, and entailing such sacrifices, cannot be well founded, and require revision* (See Appendix, page 56). The settlement of the truth here involved is a subject worthy of the professors of social science of the present time.

The insistence on this doctrine is all the more surprising because it is so utterly false in fact. The greatest variations in the relative production between gold and silver have taken place within the last two centuries, without causing any difference in the relative value between the two metals. It is true, that in the London silver market the quotations for bar silver varied by moderate percentages, but why was this so? It was due to no other cause than the shipping charges which had to be incurred for the sending away, or the purchase, of silver for India or the Continent. These shipping charges varied in percentages from time to time, and they operated in either direction. The variations caused thereby had nothing whatever to do with the production of silver, but took place in the exchange transactions on the existing stock of silver. Indeed the variations in the London prices for silver up to 1872 only proved that the bimetallic proportion of 1 to 15.5 was firmly maintained. There is nothing in the history of economics more monstrous than the use which the gold valuation party makes of the quotations of prices of silver in the London market; for these, if properly considered, prove the very contrary of the deductions usually drawn from them. (See Appendix, pages 73 and 82).

The statistics of the production of the two metals show for instance that the proportions of production of gold and silver in weight were :

In 1801 to 1810 : 1 part of gold to 50 of silver.

„ 1831 to 1840 : 1 „ „ 29 „

„ 1851 to 1860 : 1 „ „ $4\frac{1}{3}$ „

yet in spite of these almost the most extreme possible differences in the relative production, the prices of silver in London were of the respective average of 1 gold to 15.61 in the first, 15.75 in the second, and 15.76 in the third period, these slight departures from the rate of 15.5 being due to freights and charges as before stated (more complete evidence as to the matter will be found in the Appendix page 73). Even the variations which happened before the discovery of America show what the power of human legislation was able to effect in the maintenance of regular proportions (See Appendix, pages 82 to 87).

Under the light which is thus thrown upon the matter, the current saying that "a creditor is liable to be paid in the cheaper metal" also loses its commanding influence. Gold or silver, before they are coined or monetised, may be more or less cheap to the miner, just like other articles of production, of invention or of accident, are subject to labour and chance. But, when once monetised, either in coin or as Bank bars, the previous variations in original cost are once and for all neutralised. For all the subsequent holders or acquirers gold or silver have then but one fixed value. The conversion of Bank bullion into coin, or its shipment between nations, shows this in both the internal and the international trade.

In the internal intercourse, large transactions are not settled by coin, but by other methods of exchange. If anybody nevertheless has the fancy, or wants to maintain the option of receiving large sums in coin, his wish can be gratified without invalidating what is really the ordinary theory and practice. The same principle may be maintained in the international trade, but in reality a more efficacious process proceeds from the simple operation of exchanges. Under a universal agreement as to the concurrent use of gold and silver, the proportionate quantity of the two metals in each country would settle itself according to the scales of prices and other national characteristics. The richer nations would hold more gold, the others more silver.

Other minor objections have been raised to the use of silver. The principal one is that concerning its greater weight. Up to the end of last century, silver was the principal valuator of the world, and was used alongside of gold in the majority of States. It cannot surely be alleged that during this century prices in England have so far changed as to account for the abandonment of silver because its weight, as compared to value, is about 15 times that of gold. The transporting of masses of silver has been made more convenient through steam and railways; so that the conveyance from Bank to Bank as security for the issue of notes is easier. The present advance made in the clearing and banking systems almost entirely does away with the carrying about of sums of gold by individuals. Silver as well as copper coins are now carried in the pocket, and the addition thereto, or the replacement to some extent of subsidiary silver pieces by full valued silver coins, would create no inconvenience. Such minor objections of prejudice against silver, should not be allowed to influence a proper decision on the main question.

CHAPTER XVII.

The Change of Opinion which has lately manifested itself in certain directions.—The Chambers of Commerce.— The Movement in London.—The remarkable Speech of Lord Beaconsfield in 1873.—The greater readiness to Admit the Validity of the Adoption by England of the Bi-metallic System.

Although many of our old economists and other uncompromising advocates of our own system, will strenuously condemn any departure from the exclusive gold valuation, yet a considerable modification of these persistent views has lately manifested itself in other quarters. The necessity for their revision has not only been urged by a number of writers, but is now being enforced by the signs of the times and admitted by many merchants and authorities who recently have given attention to this subject. The Chambers of Commerce have occupied themselves with it. That of Liverpool waited upon the Chancellor of the Exchequer to represent the matter to him in about the same sense as it is here placed before the reader. The answer they received was not decisive, as usual in such cases. In London a strong party is being formed having the same object in view, and a petition signed by a number of first-class firms has been presented to Lord Beaconsfield, asking for a Royal Commission to inquire into the subject. A number of the members of the House of Commons begin to entertain the expediency of a change in favour of bi-metallism and even amongst our statesmen the cause is being recognised. Although Mr. Goschen adopted the attitude previously referred to at the Paris Monetary Conference, yet nothing can be more emphatic than his denunciation of the spread of the gold valuation, the demonetisation of silver, and his tacit acknowledgment of the bi-metallic system outside of England. Indeed, Mr. Goschen has entirely over-thrown the furious monometallism which has hitherto ruled either in the one or the other direction, ambiguous as his speech in the House of Commons on June 12, 1879, appears to be.

There is another authority on the subject. In November, 1873, when Mr. Disraeli was made Rector of the Glasgow University, he chose the question of valuation as his subject, and from his speech thereon, which ought to be carefully read, the following passages may be quoted :—" *I attribute the great monetary disturbance that has occurred, and is now to a certain degree acting very injuriously to trade,—I attribute it to the great changes which the Governments in Europe are making with reference to their standards of value,*" &c. Giving then an outline of what had occurred, and referring to our own system, he says, " *Now, our gold standard is, I think, a most subtle arrangement. I think that any country which has a gold standard of value should, to use a celebrated expression, think once, twice, and thrice, before it gives it up. But it is the greatest delusion in the world to attribute the commercial preponderance and prosperity of England to our having a gold standard. Our gold standard is not the* cause *of our commercial prosperity, but the* consequence *of our commercial prosperity,*" &c. He then added, " *It is quite evident we must prepare ourselves for great convulsions in the money market, not occasioned by speculation or any old cause, which has been alleged, but by a new cause with which we are not sufficiently acquainted, and the consequences of which are very embarrassing,*" &c. Alluding to the case of Germany, the means it had taken to get rid of silver to France and America, he proceeded : " *I regret to treat matters of this kind, at a moment like this, because they require to be treated with more precision of language, and with greater patience than either I or you can afford at this moment, but it did appear to me a subject to which I ought to call your attention,*" &c. And then, speaking of the spread of the gold valuation, and of the time when countries would try to get rid of silver, he says, " *Convulsions must come, and no one would be able to form an adequate idea of the monetary arrangements of the times in which he lives, if he omits from his consideration the important subject to which I have called your attention.*"

Nothing can be more striking than what was foreshadowed in this speech. The question now is :—does Lord Beaconsfield recognise that in " the cause with which we were not (in 1873) sufficiently acquainted," there is now (in 1879) more than what he then perceived, viz., that it is England especially upon whom these convulsions have the most effect ? A further question is,—Does he now perceive that the only remedy of rectifying this matter is the remonetisation of silver by England, and is he able, for the sake of this great cause, to overcome the more or less captious objections likely to be raised by the present habits and mistaken economy of the monometallic school ? For the rest, his speech does not only convey a great lesson to those who deem this subject as an unimportant one, or not connected with human legislation, but it may be said to form a pinnacle, upon which, happily or providentially, the present premier has placed himself in this matter, without reference to party.

It would now seem that the British public must come forward in order to support views to which the Government is not unwilling to listen. It remains to be seen whether the force of more reasonable opinions and national interest combined can overcome the uncompromising adherents of the gold school, so as to prepare the country for the remonetisation of silver.

CHAPTER XVIII.

The Adoption by England of a Bi-metallic System.—The addition of a Silver Piece of Four Shillings.—A Redundancy of Silver need not be feared under Universal Bi-metallism.—The Recovery in the value of Silver, and the Equity of the matter.— The Improvement of Internal Trade.—The Principle being admitted, further Improved Suggestions can be made.

What now should England do? The impression may prevail that a change in our monetary system would entail a serious disturbance of present arrangements. This is not so, the bi-metallic system may be adopted by England without involving any essential change in her present existing gold or silver coinage. Our sovereigns would continue as full legal tender; our silver coinage, from the half-crown downwards, would remain under the usual restricted rule. The only modification required in our system would be the introduction of a four-shilling piece, coined at the respective value of one part of gold to fifteen and a half of silver. Our sovereign contains 113·002 grains of *fine gold*, so this *four-shilling* piece ought to contain 350·306 grains of *fine silver*. The piece may be alloyed to the usual standard of our other silver coins, or be made nine-tenths fine, an alloy which would be less liable to abrasion. If such a piece were taken at full legal tender, this would bring about a fair bi-metallic system.

Our present system of current coinage consists of :—

Gold Sovereigns ... 20 shillings current and full metallic value.
Half Sovereigns ... 10 „ „ „ „
Silver Crowns ... 5 shillings current, but inferior token value.
Halfcrown... ... 2½ „ „ „ „
Florin ... ... 2 „ „ „ „
Shilling ... ... 1 „ „ „ „

With sixpence, fourpence, threepence and the copper coinage.

This would remain undisturbed, excepting as far as the 5s. crown-piece is concerned. This coin, although still legal, is now no longer made by the Mint, because it is too heavy. The proposed 4s. coin would modify this inconvenience ;

the present 5s. piece weighs ... ... 436·368 grains.
the proposed 4s. piece would weigh ... 381·410 grains.

of standard silver, and it would therefore be a lighter coin. It would also be more in consonance with the decimal system.

The introduction of the 4s. piece would make our system :—

Gold Sovereign	20	shillings current, and full metallic value.			
Half Sovereign	10	,,	,,	,,	,,
Silver 4s. piece	4	,,	,,	,,	,,
Half Crown	2½	shillings current, but of inferior token value.			
Florin	2	,,	,,	,,	,,
Shilling	1	,,	,,	,,	,,

With sixpence, fourpence, threepence, and the same copper coinage.

As the four-shilling piece, or British dollar, would be full legal tender in the same way as gold, the question arises whether there might not be a redundancy of them in our circulation. Under an agreement with other nations for universal bi-metallism, a redundancy of silver here need not be feared, the greater bulk of gold would remain with us, and with other countries on the same level; that of silver would drift chiefly to India, the East, and elsewhere, as it suits the lower prices and larger populations, both metals nevertheless being available for international exchange. It may be assumed that in the British Empire for instance, England would hold, say 80 per cent. of gold and 20 per cent. of silver, and India, 20 per cent. of gold and 80 per cent. of silver; other nations ranging between these proportions.

The currency of England now amounts to—

	£105	millions of gold coin in circulation.	
	30	,,	of bullion at the Bank of England (March 1879).
	18	,,	of silver change.
	1½	,,	of copper change.
Besides		£15	millions of Bank of England notes beyond the £30 millions issued on bullion (above accounted for) in reserve March, 1879.
And	...	£15·8	millions of country notes, of which perhaps,
	12	,,	are in circulation.

Total...£166½ ,, in circulation,

There would be, accordingly, in *metallic* money—

£135 millions of legal tender gold, and
18 ,, of subsidiary silver coin, or

£153 millions in gold and silver.

Now if the 4s. piece be adopted as legal tender it does not follow that therefore we should have to part with an equivalent of gold. It is certain that this piece would acquire a right of its own for internal intercourse, replacing, perhaps, a percentage of the token silver; and as it is of full metallic value any seeming surplus could always be exported. At the same time it may be mentioned (See Appendix, page 56) that the Bank of England has the right to hold a certain quantity of silver in her issue of notes. Making allowance, then, for the possible modifications, the currency of England might consist of

£100 millions of full valued gold coin in circulation,
 25 ,, of gold bullion at the Bank of England,
 20 ,, of full valued silver coin,
  5 · ,, of silver bullion at the Bank of England,
 15 ,, of silver tokens,
 1¼ ,, of copper,
     with the same amount of Bank of England notes in reserve, as before, and,
 12 ,, of country notes in circulation, besides the notes in reserve in country banks,

Total...£178½ ,, in circulation.

There would be accordingly in metallic money—

  £125 millions of legal tender gold (coin and bullion),
   25 ,,   ,, silver (coin and bullion),
   15 ,, of subsidiary silver coin,

Total...£165 millions of gold and silver.

Nobody can say that this possible modification in the component parts of our currency would affect the supremacy of gold, but it may be maintained that the additional use of silver thus made by England will greatly contribute to the recovery in its price.

The price of silver under such universal bi-metallism would speedily rise to its previous normal value, say of about 60⅞d. per oz. standard, and allowing for coinage charge, &c., the Mint price for bar silver might be determined at convenience (See Appendix, page 56). This recovery of the price of silver is a matter regarding which the opponents of the system express doubt, under the hazy notions as to the "artificiality" of the law; but those who understand what is here said, will at once see that the re-establishment of this normal price must be the natural consequence of the mints becoming open to the free coinage of silver. The suggestion that the present owners of silver would thereby make an undue profit must be set aside. As far as the huge bulk of existing coinage is concerned, which has so far suffered from the demonetisation, the re-monetisation would only equitably restore what it has lost. The same rule applies to the silver mining interest. The only parties who might profit, for the moment, would be those who had received silver bullion from mines, which at the time may be in London, but of this supply the market is often bare.

It will be seen that the adoption of the four-shilling piece would increase the circulation here. The question might therefore again be asked whether this increase here, and the re-establishment of silver through the world, would not, what is called "inflate" prices. It is evident that such a question can only be asked by the fixed income interest, which fears an increase of prices and would rather kill the goose with the golden eggs, from which that very income is derived. It is understood, of course, that prices would again rise, so as to enhance production and consumption, and restore, if not increase, the previous state of prosperity. On the other hand, the addition of such a four shilling piece to our silver coinage for internal circulation would be a great boon to the people. It is a perfectly legitimate question to ask, whether our present subsidiary silver coinage, in its extreme limitation as stated in Chapters VII. (p. 14) and IX. (p. 20), does not involve an injustice to the classes which chiefly use silver. The well-being of these classes does not alone depend upon our great industrial enterprises, for which they serve as "hands;" on which account all subsidiary or divisionary silver coinage has been designated as the "wages fund." They have an independent life and intercourse amongst themselves, for which the supply of a full-valued coin would give that expansive character to the amount of silver coinage which is now absent. (See Appendix, page 59). The bankers object to our present silver change on account of the number of different pieces and the troublesome handling of them. These four-shilling coins would be more regular, and could be dealt with easily. But the main objection of bankers to subsidiary silver is due to their inability to pay it away, or to export it, whenever they happen to have a surplus in hand. Any surplus of full-valued four-shilling pieces could be exported without loss, and their use would tend to lessen the amount of the token silver.

Upon the recognition of the simple matters here involved, England might enter into a fresh international conference for the purposes of general agreement, when it may nevertheless be possible to modify the proposal made, in the manner to be shown in the next chapters.

CHAPTER XIX.

The suitability of such a Dollar on behalf of India.—The Means of Introducing the £ into India.—Conversion of the Indian System in prospect.

Were England willing to promote an international conference she might claim a special arrangement on behalf of India. The strict adherence to the bi-metallic proportion of 1 to 15½ requires the four-shilling piece of 350.305 grains of pure silver, but this would not fit the Indian rupee of 165 grains fine. The gold mohur being unsuitable, it would be necessary then for the effective introduction of a gold piece into India to choose a coin of 10 rupees to contain 106.452 fine grains. A proposal may however be made which, whilst bringing our English system into immediate accord with that of India, and tending to the introduction of our sovereign into that colony, would satisfy the universal bi-metallic agreement, and might, under certain conditions, absolve us from the immediate abandonment of our gold valuation.

Instead of coining a four-shilling piece of 350.306 grains fine silver, let this piece contain 350.625 grains.

The Indian rupee contains   165   grains = 16 annas ;
the new piece would contain 350.625 grains = 34 annas.
this new piece thus being worth = 2 rupees 2 annas precisely.

Such a piece might be coined for India in addition to the present rupee, and in full accord with it, without requiring any other change in the Indian silver coinage. Rupees and their sub-divisons might be coined as before, but instead of coining none but rupees, let a certain amount be coined in these 2 rupees 2 anna pieces. The Indian bazaar people, would refuse a piece of 350.305 grains, as inexact, but would recognise that this piece of 350.625 grains was in exact accordance with the existing Indian laws, whether it be alloyed to the Indian standard, or nine-tenths fine. The piece would be of the favourite dollar type, and might command the East and Africa as a British dollar. At the same time, this piece should be coined in England, to circulate here as a four-shilling piece. If that were done, five of these pieces would be equal to £1, and thus the way for the introduction of that gold coin into India would be paved. It may be some time before the sovereign thus forms an integral part of Indian currency; but it is more than likely that it would soon make its way in a manner sufficient to serve for exchanges.

The Indian Currency might thus consist of :

Gold Sovereigns of 20 Shillings, or 5 Dollars = 170 Annas.
Half Sovereigns „ 10 „ „ 2½ „ = 85 „
Silver Dollars „ 4 „ 1 „ = 34 „
Rupees ... ... = 16 „
½ Rupee ... ... = 8 „
¼ Rupee ... = 4 „
⅛ Rupee ... = 2 „
Copper coins—3 Pice⎫
    „   1 Pice⎬ 1 Anna being = 12 Pice.

The relative agreement between these figures would not be more inconvenient then the now existing proportions. The rupee at 16 annas of 12 pice has 192 pice, in itself an awkward number. The proposed dollar would have precisely 408 pice, a more convenient division for ultimate conversion into 400 pice.

The present currency of India, apart from the note circulation of about £6 millions, if taken at nearly £200 millions, might then be gradually modified by lesser coinage of rupees, and by more of dollars. The introduction of gold sovereigns being rendered easier through these dollars, the coinage of India in a few years hence might be :—

Gold Sovereigns and Half Sovereigns £30 millions
Silver Dollars ... ... 70 „
Rupee coinage and subdivisions ... 100 „

At some later time, when the number of rupees might be further reduced by conversion into the new coin, half dollars could also be issued. Finally, it would be possible to convert a moderate quantity of the lower silver coinage, from the quarter dollar downwards, into tokens of the same value as our own shilling and its subdivisions, into subsidiary pieces. The £ being now equivalent to 2,040 pice, a copper piece of the value of 2 pice would be at the rate of 1,020 to the £, and the reduction of this to the rate of 1,000 to the £ could easily be effected. It may be stated that the German Government has recently reduced the ⅓ thaler from 120 to 100 pfennige, without any inconvenience being experienced, and similar operations have been performed in other instances. These 2 pice pieces might then be called farthings, and at some future time the Indian coinage might appear as :—

Full Valued Coin.

Gold Sovereign = 5 Dollars = 20 Shillings = 1,000 Farthings.

„ Half Sovereign = 2½ „ = 10 „ = 500 „

Silver Dollar or Double Rupee 4 „ = 200 „

„ Half Dollar or New Rupee ... 2 „ = 100 „

Subsidiary Coin.

Silver Shilling or Half Rupee ... ... = 50 Farthings.

„ Four-tenths of a Shilling ... ... = 20 „

„ Two-tenths „ ... ... = 10 „

Copper—One Penny ... ... = 4 „

„ Halfpenny ... ... = 2 „

„ Farthing ... ... = 1 „

„ Pice ... ... = ¼ „

and smaller pieces if required. The decimalization of the £1 into 1,000 pieces of 2 pice each can thus be accomplished. A new division to replace the Anna can, if necessary, be found.

This would become the true Anglo-Indian system, towards which we might aim· With the addition of Banknotes, founded on an effective store of gold and silver, there might then be in use in India after a few years :—

Full valued gold coin and bullion ... £40 milions⎫ Full legal

„ silver coin and bullion ... 140 „ ⎬ tender.

Subsidiary silver tokens ... ... 20 „ ⎫ Limited

Copper tokens ... ... 3 „ ⎬ tender.

This reform is entirely practicable without recourse to any forcible measures. That this is so is evident from the fact that there would be no pressing necessity to carry it all out at once, because the proposed 4s. piece can be used alongside of the present rupee coinage for as long as may be deemed proper. The importance of this proposal as connected with the general question will be made evident in the next chapter.

CHAPTER XX.

The Agreement of this Arrangement with the Bi-metallic Systems.—It is favourable to England.—England's possible Adherence to the Gold Valuation.—The Equilibrium might, nevertheless, be Restored.—But England's Interests demand an Agreement.

The arrangement suggested in the foregoing chapter would seem to rest on the English and Indian systems alone, without any reference to other nations. But it also so happens, that at the respective proportions of fine gold in the sovereign and of fine silver in the proposed dollar, the rate between the two metals would be as 1 to 15.515, the bi-metallic proportion being 1 to 15·5. The small difference, equal to a margin of nearly one per Mille (or one-tenth of 1 per cent.) on the proportion between the two, would be tantamount to a slight handicap in favour of gold on our part, sufficient in common arbitrations of exchanges, to guard us effectually against redundancy in silver. Foreign nations, if a set-off be deemed requisite, in their turn, might make a slight increase in the charge for coining silver. It is evident, then, that such a piece of 350.625 grains in pure silver is the proper thing to adopt, even if England contemplates to take to full bi-metallism. It might be expedient to make this piece of the fineness of 900, so that its full weight would be 389.583 grains troy.

A further question might now be asked on behalf of England. This question is, whether this silver piece should be at once full legal tender in the United Kingdom or not. If its tender, like that of our present silver coins, were limited to £2, England would not give up her gold valuation. But England might, nevertheless, absorb say £10 or £12 millions of such pieces for internal circulation. For although the legal tender would be so limited, there is every probability that a much larger amount of this coin would be used than of the old five shilling pieces. The fact that the new coins would be of full value and exportable, does away with two of the three severe restrictions upon our silver coinage spoken of in Chapters II. and VII., and thus a larger amount could be used without involving loss to bankers, and without creating redundancy. To a certain extent, these pieces would attain a character not unlike that of the use which the Germans made of gold under their previous silver valuation. Although gold in Germany had no legal tender at all, yet nearly 20 per cent. of her monetary circulation consisted of gold coins of all sorts. This four shilling piece having, at all events, a legal tender right to £2 here in England, might therefore obtain a safer footing. Those who fully appreciate this question of the valuation, with its strong contrast between the treatment of gold and silver in the gold system, may be able to see that this proposal contains a *principle of reconciliation between these contrasts*, which will promote the use of silver without invalidating the gold valuation. Indeed, if the tender of such silver were extended to £5 or £10, or to any higher reasonable amount short of full legal tender, the main principle of the gold system would remain. At the same time, in either case, the Bank of England would be able to use her right of holding a certain proportion of silver in her issue department, as a store against Indian demand. (See Appendix, page 56). The four shilling pieces might be coined here for India, and would, no doubt, drift in that direction, as silver bars have hitherto done, and as under the revival of trade, they would do in an increased proportion.

If England came forward with such a proposal, Germany might be willing to treat her remaining stock of silver thalers in the same way, and such joint action would go far to restore the lost equilibrium. And if besides France, and America, other nations joined the existing bi-metallic group, the *equilibrium would be completely restored,* so that the latter would be able to resume the free coinage of silver.

It is expedient, perhaps, that England should reserve to herself this position for the present, so as to satisfy the scruples of the gold party, on the plea of old contracts. For, although under a bi-metallic arrangement, the paying of the creditor in either gold or silver would not result in any loss whatever to him, yet a certain time might be permitted to elapse, for the purpose of allowing mercantile engagements to be contracted for upon the full bi-metallic basis. A further legitimate reason for the form of this proposal lies in the fact that it will take some time before India attains a fair bi-metallic system, and that England may occupy an intermediate position of reserve with a view to better maintaining the equilibrium, until India is further advanced, and can make and receive effective gold remittances. It is better also that for the present the issue of the pieces here should be under Government, like the rest of our silver coinage. At any time then, hereafter, all that is required, if need be, would be the extension of the legal tender right of this proposed four shilling piece up to the full legal tender, and to allow its free coinage. The suggestion made, therefore, involves not a mere expedient, but principles which England might plead before another International conference, and which may be loyally and fairly discussed. But should such conference, nevertheless, demand the adoption by England of the full bi-metallic system, it would be her interest to conform thereto.

Finally, whatever scheme is to be adopted, whether full bi-metallism at once or the modification above suggested, it will be obvious that our Government must act speedily and energetically. Every week which is lost adds to the irreconcilable differences and losses betwixt England and India, to the loss of our home industry, and steadily increases the necessity under which foreign nations are placed to manufacture their own goods. England, therefore, should assist in promoting another international monetary conference before it is too late. At such conference more reasonable views may prevail, and the leading nations can bring to bear the forces of intelligence, as well as those of coercion in commercial policy. In an age like the present, when communication between distant nations for the exchange of ideas, as well as commodities, is far more rapid than was formerly the case between neighbouring towns, an international understanding on such a point as this is demanded in the interests of peace by every principle on which civilization is founded. To us in England this is not a mere matter of sentimentality, but it is dictated to us by the actual situation in which we find ourselves, and in view of which we have always legitimately urged on other nations the acceptance of maxims of trade which we deem of value to humanity at large. The present occasion is the great test which will decide whether the statesmen, the economists, and the strata of society usually entrusted with the business of ruling, irrespective of party divisions in politics, be it here in England or in foreign countries, are fit to act in this overwhelmingly important matter for the national and general welfare.

APPENDIX.

To Chapter XI.—"*More than three-fourths of England's outward trade is conducted on the silver basis. The exports to countries on the gold valuation basis have increased in the usual satisfactory manner, but those to countries with the silver valuation have all the more declined.*"

In the Table and Statements here following, the changes which have taken place in the exports of the produce of the United Kingdom, from 1874 to 1878 (both inclusive) are shown. The countries are grouped so as to indicate the systems of valuations to which they respectively belong. The nations are designated as they generally appeared in the year 1874, *i.e.*, in the then existing state of valuation. In that year, for instance, Germany began active sales of silver, but was still on the silver basis, whilst now, in 1879, she has completed her gold system to the extent of say, three-fourths; so, with Holland and other States, she is placed under the "silver systems, *changing to gold.*" Again, such a State as Chili, for example, under the "bi-metallic States," appears yet as "*silver predominating,*" although, within the last two years an enforced paper currency had to be resorted to. It is obvious that, for the purpose in view, the condition of matters as it was nearest to 1874 must be the starting point. The terms "*fully effective,*" "*defective,*" "*nominal,*" "*under paper-issue,*" etc., will be understood. It remains to be remarked that among the gold-valuation States, for instance, Canada is entirely "nominal," and that by placing it under the category of gold, the table gives it a classification hardly deserved. The notes attached at the end of the tables give further accounts of the various systems. The table begins with the year 1874, although the decline of trade dates from the close of 1872. The year 1872 is generally called the year of the hey-day of British commerce, and although there was no valid occasion (excepting the demonetisation of silver) for the non-increase, and still less for the reduction since, yet, as the above real cause did not become alarmingly effective until 1874, that year is selected as the already modified basis to start from. It must, however, be borne in mind that in 1872 and 1873, the demonetisation of silver, initiated by Germany, already caused sensible disturbances in the general aspect of international trade, first encouraging large shipments of goods to the East, and curtailing the continental and other trades, the falling of between 1872 and 1874 being £16,403,000.

TABLE.—Shewing the amount of exports of British and Irish produce to Foreign Countries and to British possessions, from 1874 to 1878, and the increase or decrease between the years 1874 and 1878 ; the countries being grouped under their respective systems of valuations. The numbers under " Notes for reference " (first column) refer to explanations which follow as necessary to each country.

Notes for Reference.	Systems of Valuation in Countries.	1874.	1875.	1876.	1877.	1878.	Plus or Minus, in £ sterling (full) in 1878.	+ or − per cent. in 1878.
				In £ sterling, 000 being omitted.				
	GOLD VALUATIONS—							
	Fully effective.							
1	Australia and New Zealand	19,064,	19,483,	17,675,	19,286,	19,570,	Plus £506,000	+ 2,7 °/₀
2	South African Settlements	4,848,	5,264,	4,711,	4,608,	5,320,	,, 472,000	+ 9,7 ,,
	Defective and mixed.							
3	Channel Islands	817,	641,	586,	555,	535,	Minus 282,000	− 34,6 ,,
4	Malta and Gozo	822,	700,	894,	819,	1,160,	Plus 338,000	+ 41,1 ,,
5	Portugal and Azores	3,057,	2,790,	2,408,	2,425,	2,224,	Minus 833,000	− 27,0 ,,
6	Persia	38,	47,	71,	158,	149,	Plus 111,000	+ 292,1 ,,
	Nominal.							
7	North American Colonies	11.419,	9,029,	7,358,	7,614,	6,412,	Minus 5,007,000	− 43,8 ,,
	Under Paper Issue.							
8	Brazil	7,678,	6,867,	5,920,	5,958,	5,580,	,, 2,098,000	− 27,3 ,,
9	Argentine Confederation	3,128,	2,388,	1,543,	2,092,	2,312,	,, 816,000	− 26,1 ,,
10	Turkey	8,283,	6,939,	6,630,	5,822,	8,646,	Plus 363,000	+ 4,4 ,,
	GOLD & SILVER VALUATIONS (Bimetalliam).							
	Fully effective.							
11	France	14,448,	15,340,	16,086,	14,233,	14,819,	,, 371,000	+ 2,6 ,,
12	Belgium	5,828,	5,784,	5,875,	5,304,	5,525,	Minus 303,000	− 5,2 ,,
	Silver Predominating.							
13	Spain and the Canaries	4,262,	3,625,	4,140,	3,809,	3,374,	,, 888,000	− 20,8 ,,
14	Gibraltar	1,135,	969,	1,121,	869,	711,	,, 424,000	− 37,4 ,,
15	Phillipine Islands, &c.	962,	930,	727,	1,292,	836,	,, 126,000	− 13,1 ,,
16	Spanish and French West Indies	1,921,	2,779,	2,131,	2,424,	2,079,	Plus 158,000	+ 8,2 ,,
17	Algeria	48,	156,	210,	271,	169,	,, 121,000	+ 252,1 ,,
18	Venezuela	506,	733,	679,	620,	474,	Minus 32,000	− 6,3 ,,
19	United States of Columbia	1,541,	917,	783,	912,	1,032,	,, 509,000	− 33,0 ,,
20	Chili	2,751,	2,215,	1,916,	1,501,	1,191,	,, 1,560,000	− 56,7 ,,
	Fairly Effective.							
21	Japan	2,030,	2,463,	2,033,	2,203,	2,616,	Plus 586,000	+ 29,0 ,,
	Under Paper Issue.							
22	Greece	1,010,	980,	867,	867,	981,	Minus 29,000	− 2,9 ,,
23	Italy	6,370,	6,765,	6,689,	6,219,	5,350,	,, 1,020,000	− 16,0 ,,
24	Uruguay	1,224,	713,	1,006,	1,078,	999,	,, 225,000	− 18,4 ,,
	Special.							
25	United States of America	26,155,	21,874,	16,834,	16,377,	14,616,	,, 11,539,000	− 44,1 ,,
	SILVER VALUATIONS—							
	Changing to Gold since 1872.							
26	Germany	24,800,	23,290,	20,082,	19,642,	19,460,	Minus 5,340,000	− 21,5 ,,
27	Denmark	2,520,	2,324,	2,195,	1,828,	1,533,	,, 987,000	− 39,2 ,,
28	Sweden and Norway	5,401,	4,538,	4,225,	4,180,	2,801,	,, 2,600,000	− 48,1 ,,
29	Holland	14,427,	13,122,	11,777,	9,614,	9,291,	,, 5,136,000	− 35,6 ,,
	Effective.							
30	Mexico, Central America	1,955,	1,975,	1,641,	2,274,	1,776,	,, 179,000	− 9,1 ,,
31	Danish West Indies	341,	379,	257,	225,	238,	,, 103,000	− 30,2 ,,
32	Dutch West Indies	223,	153,	81,	93,	146,	,, 77,000	− 34,5 ,,
33	French and Dutch Guiana	45,	26,	29,	43,	40,	,, 5,000	− 11,1 ,,
34	British West Indies, &c.	3,449,	3,129,	3,067,	3,027,	2,783,	,, 666,000	− 19,3 ,,
	Fairly Effective.							
35	Egypt	3,220,	2,946,	2,630,	2,273,	2,195,	,, 1,025,000	− 31,8 ,,
36	Tripoli and Tunis	102,	122,	65,	38,	45,	,, 57,000	− 56,0 ,,
37	Morocco	443,	343,	396,	393,	191,	,, 252,000	− 56,9 ,,
	Fully Effective.							
38	China (exclusive of Hong Kong)	5,406,	4,928,	4,611,	4,404,	3,725,	,, 1,681,000	− 31,1 ,,
39	Hong Kong	3,476,	3,598,	3,080,	3,508,	2,871,	,, 605,000	− 17,4 ,,
40	British India, &c.	27,865,	27,291,	25,448,	28,660,	25,853,	,, 2,002,000	− 7,2 ,,
41	Java, &c.	1,572,	1,577,	1,562,	1,907,	1,456,	,, 116,000	− 7,4 ,,
	Under Paper Issue.							
42	Austria	1,064,	906,	785,	1,042,	760,	,, 304,000	− 28,6 ,
43	Russia	8,776,	8,081,	6,193,	4,179,	6,524,	,, 2,252,000	− 226,2 ,,
44	Peru	1,593,	1,591,	991,	1,266,	1,369,	,, 224,000	− 14,1 ,,
45	Hayti, &c.	442,	693,	356,	383,	333,	,, 109,000	− 24,7 ,,
	BARTER TRADE—							
	Or indefinable Valuations.							
46	West Coast of Africa	937,	798,	909,	1,177,	1,174,	Plus 237,000	+ 25,3 ,
47	West African Colonies.	882,	789,	742,	840,	897,	,, 15,000	+ 1,7 ,,
48	East Coast of Africa	53,	154,	134,	166,	213,	,, 160,000	+ 302,0 ,,
49	Other Places	478,	400,	376,	415,	450,	Minus 28,000	− 5,8 ,,
50	In transit to other destinations	743,	—	—	—	—		
	TOTALS	£239,558,	£223,494,	£200,639,	£198,893,	£192,804		

RECAPITULATION.

In £ Sterling, 000 being omitted.

INCREASE IN EXPORTS.			Exports in 1874.	Exports in 1878.	Per centage plus.
GOLD VALUATION	Fully effective...	Australia and New Zealand	19,064,	19,570,	+ 2,7 °/₀
		South African Settlements ...	4,848,	5,320,	+ 9,7 ,,
	Mixed ...	Malta and Gozo	822,	1,160,	+ 41,1 ,,
		Persia...	38,	149,	+ 292,1 ,,
	Under paper issue	Turkey	8,283,	8,646,	+ 4,4 ,,
BI-METALLISM	Fully effective...	France	14,448,	14,819,	+ 2,6 ,,
	Effective	Algeria	48,	169,	+ 250,1 ,,
		Spanish and French West Indies	1,921,	2,079,	+ 8,2 ,,
	Fairly effective	Japan ...	2,080,	2,616,	+ 20,0 ,,
BARTER TRADE	Indefinable systems	West Coast of Africa	937,	1,174,	+ 25,3 ,,
		West African Colonies	882,	897,	+ 1,7 ,,
		East Coast of Africa...	53,	213,	+ 302,0 ,,
		Totals	£53,374,	£66,812,	+ 6,4 °/₀

DECREASE IN EXPORTS.			Exports in 1874.	Exports in 1878.	Per centage minus.
GOLD VALUATION	Defective	Channel Islands	817,	535,	— 34,6 °/₀
		Portugal and Azores...	3,057,	2,324,	— 27,0 ,,
	Nominal	North American Colonies	11,410,	6,412,	— 43,8 ,,
	Under paper issue	Brazil ...	7,678,	5,580,	— 27,3 ,,
		Argentine Confederation	3,128,	2,312,	— 26,1 ,,
BI-METALLISM	Fully effective...	Belgium	5,828,	5,525,	— 5,2 ,,
	Silver predominating...	Spain and the Canaries	4,262,	3,374,	— 20,8 ,,
		Gibraltar	1,135,	711,	— 37.4 ,,
		Phillipine Islands, &c.	962,	836,	— 13,1 ,,
		Venezuela	506,	474,	— 6,3 ,,
		United States of Columbia ...	1,541,	1,032,	— 33,0 ,,
		Chili	2,751,	1,191,	— 56,7 ,,
	Under paper issue	Greece...	1,010,	981,	— 2,9 ,,
		Italy ...	6,370,	5,350,	— 16,0 ,,
		Uruguay	1,224,	999,	— 18,4 ,,
	Special	United States of America ...	26,155,	14,616,	— 44,1 ,,
SILVER VALUATIONS	Changing to gold	Germany	24,800,	19,460,	— 21,6 ,
		Denmark	2,520,	1,533,	— 39,2 ,,
		Sweden and Norway	5,401,	2,801,	— 48,1 ,,
		Holland	14,427,	9,291,	— 35,6 ,,
	Effective	Mexico, Central America	1,955,	1,776,	— 9,1 ,,
		Danish West Indies ...	341,	238,	— 30,2 ,,
		Dutch West Indies ...	223,	146,	— 34,5 ,,
		French and Dutch Guiana ...	45,	40,	— 11,1 ,,
		British West Indies, &c.	3,449,	2,783,	— 19,3 ,,
	Fairly effective	Egypt ...	3,220,	2, 95,	— 31,8 ,,
		Tripoli and Tunis	102,	45,	— 56,0 ,,
		Morocco	413,	191,	— 66,2 ,,
	Fully effective...	China (exclusive of Hong Kong)	5,406,	3,725,	— 31,1 ,,
		Hong Kong	3,476,	2,871,	— 17,3 ,,
		British India, &c.	27,866,	25,853,	— 7,2 ,,
		Java, &c.	1,572,	1,456,	— 7,4 ,,
	Under paper issue	Austria	1,064,	760,	— 28,6 ,,
		Russia...	8,776,	6 524,	— 26,2 ,,
		Peru ...	1,593,	1,369,	— 14,1 ,,
		Hayti, &c.	442,	333,	— 24,7 ,,
	Other places	Various	478,	450,	— 5,8 ,,
		In transit to other destinations	743,	—	—
		Totals	£186,184,	£135,091,	— 27 °/₀

Increase on

Gold systems ...	£33,055,	to	£34,845,	or plus 5.4 per cent.
Bi-metallism ...	18,447,	,,	19,683,	,, 6.7 ,,
Barter trade ...	1,874,	,,	2,284,	,, 21.9 ,,

Decrease on

Defective, &c., gold ...	26,099,	,,	17,063,	or minus 34.6 ,,
Bi-metallism ...	51,744,	,,	35,089,	,, 32.2 ,,
Silver systems ...	108,341,	,,	84,840,	,, 21.7 ,,

And if India be set apart, as having been subject to rather larger speculative shipments, the decline on the rest of the silver States is about 30.4 per cent.

These statements speak for themselves. They show conclusively that the increase in the Exports of British produce has taken place only with countries who either have the fully effective gold system, or the bi-metallic system in which

E

gold predominates; or, as in the case of Turkey, under exceptional circumstances. On the other hand, the gold valuation States, whose system is defective, nominal, or under paper-issue, the bi-metallic countries whose system is not so effective as others, together with the special case of the United States, show a serious decline. All the silver valuing countries, however, without exception, show a continuous decrease.

Making allowance for the share which bimetallism has in gold, and including this under the head of *gold interest*, also, on the other hand, including the defective systems and the share which bimetallism has in silver, under the head of *silver interest*, the entire case can be simplified, and placed under these *two main* heads, as follows :—

From the Year 1874 to 1878,

Increase on British export on the *gold interest*
£53,374,000 to £56,812,000 ...   ...   or 6.4 per cent.
Decrease of British exports on the *silver interest*
£184,852,000 to £135,992,000   ...   .   or 26.4   ,,
But if the trade with the same States as grouped in the Table on page 49 is taken at its aggregate in 1872, we have

From 1872 to 1878,

Increase on British exports on the *gold interest*
£52,068,000 to £56,812,000 ...   ...   or 9.1   ,,
Decrease on British exports on the *silver interest*
£203,893,000 to £135,992,000   ...   .   or 33.3   ,,
The latter being the minus percentage on 1872, equal to a plus percentage of 50 per cent. on 1878.

In the present year (1879) the first two months (January and February) show a further decline, as against the corresponding months of 1878, of about 10 per cent., the greater part being found assignable to countries interested in silver. For the purposes of account, the difference as above pointed out ought to be increased by about 11 per cent. on account of freight and charges. Our shipping interest has been so much less even without references to much lower rates of freight, &c.

The above statement refers only to the exports of the produce of the United Kingdom, without reference to foreign goods re-exported. The question of imports would be an interesting one to deal with, but space is not available here for that purpose. On this subject reference may be made to "The Wealth of Nations and the Question of Silver," published by Eden Fisher & Co., 50, Lombard Street.

The following are the special notes referring to their corresponding number under "reference to notes" in the table (page 48). (For dates of Monetary Laws and Coinages of various nations see *Parliamentary Report on the Depreciation of Silver, Appendix, pp.* 2—9.) :—

1. The Australian colonies, as a matter of course, have the fully effective gold valuation, not only as gold producing countries, but on a legal basis identical with that of England.
2. The South African colonies are also on the fully effective system, although in the neighbourhood various silver dollars are dealt in.
3. The Channel Islands have our system legally, but a good deal of French money is in circulation, and their currency matters have special local features.
4. The increase in the trade of Malta and Gozo in 1878 is no doubt chiefly due to the war in the East. The silver scudo is still a unit of value.

5. Portugal has a defective gold valuation. Although gold is legal tender, yet she coins no gold, but uses British sovereigns in moderate quantities, and otherwise the silver milreis system reigns.

6. Persia has a partially effective gold valuation, but has only a small stock of gold.

7. In the North American colonies the sovereign is legal tender, but together with the United States' coin, it is valued by tariff, and the dollar system, represented by bank notes generally, renders the gold valuation quite nominal. These colonies are so closely allied to the commerce of the United States that their recent strong protective tendency is a bitter sarcasm on the tenacity of England as regards the question before us. This defiance of the mother country, the champion of free trade, is also mainly due to England herself having helped to destroy the basis of international currency; and it will be interesting to watch the conflict in prospect between the home government, and the interest which the colonial authorities deem necessary to defend.

8 and 9. The Brazils and the Argentine Confederation labour under a depreciated paper currency, and find the greatest difficulty in returning to specie payments. Their gold valuation is worse than nominal.

10. Turkey is in the most hopeless state of bankruptcy and paper issue, and although the increase in 1878 was partly due to the war, yet it is a most remarkable feature that Turkey, since she does no longer pay interest on her debts, is rather increasing her imports. This is a striking illustration of the truth of the remarks made in Chapter XII. as to the "fresh basis" upon which defaulting nations are thus placed.

11. France has the full bi-metallic system, with a preponderance of gold. As is now so well known, her bi-metallic system has hitherto been the compensatory machinery through which the English and Indian valuations were able to exchange. It is true, that thereby, some part of the silver coinage left France, but the amount of gold which the country, through her balance of trade, has acquired, is perhaps five times as large. Within the last few years, much of the French silver, not melted down abroad, has returned, and the Bank of France holds more than £40 millions in its vaults, there being besides an amount of nearly £70 millions of 5 franc pieces in circulation. France will, no doubt, adhere to her bi-metallic system as long as she can, but ultimately, if silver be not remonetised, she will not be able to continue on that footing.

12. Belgium has the same system, but with less gold, and her State bank is rather weak in gold bullion. Her strong disposition to adopt the gold valuation is likely to be practically checked by the large amount of Belgian 5 franc pieces coined in accordance with the Latin union, for which she is responsible. The comparative regularity of her trade, during the last five years, is however, noteworthy. The absurdity of the allegation that the competition of foreign nations is the cause of the decline in our exports, is especially illustrated here. France and Belgium are the countries whose competition with us is the most keen; yet our exports to France itself have increased, and those to Belgium remain steady, in spite of the complaints of both nations as to the dulness of their own export and home trade.

13. Spain has the bi-metallic system, fairly effective, but weaker than the two preceding countries. Nevertheless the recent reform in her currency system, and the establishment of a central Bank are likely much to fortify and improve her metallic monetary system; and if silver were remonetised, our trade and other financial relations with her would be much improved.

14. In Gibraltar the £ sterling is legal tender, but the dollar prevails, and on account of its proximity to Spain, it is properly placed into her category.

15. The Phillipine and Ladrone islands have the Spanish valuation, with silver predominating.

16. With the Spanish and French West Indies there is a slight increase of trade.

17. Algeria has the same system as France.

18. Venezuela has kept its bi-metallic system in a fair state, but through the demonetisation of silver, her valuation has become affected.

19. In the United States of Columbia the singular feature again appears, that although some states of the confederacy have ceased to pay interest on its loans, the trade within the last three or four years has increased.

20. Chili has the bi-metallic system, but of late years silver predominated, and at the present time there are indications which place the country amongst the depreciated paper valuing states.

21. Japan, since the trade was open, first adopted the gold valuation, but subsequently re-introduced the silver Yen, on the bi-metallic system. The increase in our trade with her is no doubt due to the rapid strides she makes in civilisation.

22, 23, and 24. These are States under an old paper valuation still depreciated, and have no metallic currency; in Italy, even the fractional currency is paper.

25. The United States, marked as "special," show a large decrease, due partly to other causes than that of the demonetisation of silver. Nevertheless, if silver were remonetised, and the United States were able to send us that metal in exchange, the previous state of trade would be regained, and perhaps exceeded. During the last two years, America has forwarded but very little silver to Europe, and it has been said that its Western Mines show signs of exhaustion. That is not the case. Only those mines which do not contain silver combined with gold are standing still at present. The outlay, in wages, &c., on these poor ores, is rather large, and as their energetic working would tend much to lower the price in Europe, it is the policy to cease working for the present.

26. Germany has exchanged about two-thirds of her silver for gold, and still holds the other third, to be demonetised, in abeyance. It must be borne in mind that, but for the £200,000,000 received from France, Germany would have been quite unable to have changed her valuation. The decline of our trade with her, from 1874, is 21¼ per cent.; from 1872 to 1878 is at the rate of about 35 per cent. The protectionist tendency shewn by Germany is due principally to her inability to hold the gold acquired; for not only does her export trade suffer from the same causes as ours, but the surrounding States thereby draw upon her for gold.

27 and 28.—In the Scandinavian union the gold valuation has been legally introduced, but remains as yet ineffective because they have not the means of acquiring much gold, and use paper currency chiefly.

29. Holland, up to 1872 a silver country, has also made gold legal, and acquired a certain portion,

but still holds almost the whole of her silver. The decline in the last four years is at the rate of 35·6 per cent Since 1872 the decline amounts to 43 per cent. In note 41, referring to her Eastern possession, Java, this decline will again be referred to.

30 to 34. This group of States, although some little gold is current, is on the silver basis, and even in the British West Indies, the dollar rules.

35 to 37. These States make use of some gold, but in Morocco and Tunis the valuation is legally and preponderately silver. The decline in the Egyptian trade during the last three years is not so serious as her financial difficulties would lead to suppose it should be.

38 and 39. China is a silver country *par excellence*. The trade in small gold bars and gold leaf does not interfere with the absolute supremacy of silver, and the decline in our trade with her since 1872 is nearly 44 per cent. Considering that Europe, and especially England, is such a large consumer of Chinese goods, the remarkable stoppage in the trade with China, is one of the most significant signs of its real cause.

40. The trade with British India since 1874 has only declined by about 7 per cent. in 1878. But this must by no means be taken as a less discouraging sign. In the first place, a great proportion of our manufacturing concerns at home are permanently established for the Indian trade, and had to continue business. In that they were encouraged by the rise and fall in the price of silver, engendering a great deal of speculation, and overstocking of the Indian markets. The decline, therefore, ought not to be measured by the ·figures here submitted, but the heavy losses incurred on the exports to India during the last few years ought to be added. What these are, cannot be estimated, but they have, so to speak, nearly ruined those participating in her trade in this country.

41. Java is a Dutch possession, and offers the most remarkable example of what bi-metallism can do on behalf of a colony. Whilst the rupee in India has declined by 25 or more per cent., and the exchange fallen from say 2s. to 1s. 7d., the Dutch florin and the Java exchange remain unaltered, and our trade with Java has suffered but a moderate decline. The reason is obvious. The parent country, Holland, although hitherto under a silver valuation, has adopted gold as legal tender in the bi-metallic proportion of 1 to 15½; so that the exchange between Holland and England, for instance, remains at its par of about £1 to 12 Dutch florins. Therefore, whether Java remits produce or florins to Holland or England, or England be paid in drafts on Holland, there is no loss whatever in the exchange. Holland, as a matter of course, has ceased to coin silver as full legal tender, and keeps what she has got provisionally, and for the trade between herself and Java; but as far as she herself is concerned, she is bound to procure as much gold as possible—*i.e.*, to keep the exchange in her favour at all hazards, and this she can only do by importing less from England and other countries. Hence the decline of our trade with Holland referred to in Note 29.

42. Austria is under an old paper valuation on the silver basis, although her exchange with England and other countries, hovers about a doubtful gold point. She has lately purchased silver because the decline in its price exceeded the depreciation of her exchange, so that shipments of silver to Vienna paid a margin. But not only has this produced a reaction on the exchange, but the Austrian Government contemplates stopping the free coinage of silver, rather than substitute one depreciated currency for another. And only in the case of the remonetisation of silver can Austria derive any benefit from that metal.

43. Russia's paper valuation is a great drawback to the trade of other countries with her. British commerce with her and the far East would be much enhanced if silver were remonetised.

44. Peru has been plunged into a paper valuation, but it is again a singular fact that, since she ceased to pay interest on her debt, our export trade with her has increased by about 38 per cent.

45. Hayti is in a state of abject dependence on a paper valuation.

46, 47, and 48. The trade on the African coasts is essentially a barter trade ; and it is worthy of notice that this exhibits a large increase.

49. Other places refer to small exports not worthy of comment.

50. In transitu. In the years 1873-1874, the monthly and quarterly returns, from which these statistics are taken, state items in transit through various countries for other destinations, most of which·were accounted for, but the balance noted under this item is not so traceable. In order to forestall mistaken criticism, it must here be stated, for instance, that in the yearly returns for the United States for 1874, there is included the transit to Canada, &c., so that these annual returns differ from the monthly returns. Since the year 1875, however, this method has been abandoned, and the true destinations are indicated. In the preceding accounts this item is not included, but as the goods went chiefly to silver countries, it adds a small per centage against the silver interest.

The foregoing tables and the notes following thereon contain as complete a survey of the condition of the export trade of the produce of the United Kingdom, and the state of the valuations of the various countries, as can be given in so small a space. It is a pity that as regards these valuations, *i.e.*, their proportionate divisions, their variations in effectiveness, down to the paper issue of the lowest class, there prevails in this country so little accurate knowledge. But those who are able, from the matter here laid before them, to gain some idea of these various actual conditions, may also perceive how closely these correspond with the actual results of trade.

Among the lessons which the tables convey are these : wars have not caused the decline, for in present times they seem to enhance trade.—The allegation that the present state is but a phase in a "cycle" in trade, already disproved in Chapter VIII., is further refuted by the fact that decline has taken place only in the case of the silver interest.—The cessation of foreign loans has little to do with the matter, for not only is the decline in our export trade far in excess of our capacity to grant loans, even in the most prosperous times, but our trade has fallen off, especially with nations which do not require loans from us ; while nations which have failed to pay interest on their loans, seem to take rather more goods from us than before.—That strikes and foreign competition, whether supposed to be engendered thereby or not, have not caused the decline is clear ; for not only do strikes take place abroad, but the foreign manufacturer complains of English competition in both his home and outward trade.—Indeed no nation can as yet successfully compete with England in manufacturing cheaply and effectively.—Nor is this a case of England's "overproduction ;" for this production has already lessened through lower prices. But, in spite of lower prices, there lies in this matter of "the decline in the power of payment," the cause of the "under-consumption" enforced upon the world by the demonetisation of silver, the sole and original cause of all the mischief done and in prospect. If this cannot be recognised from the statements and statistics submitted, there is an end to all rhyme and reason in this important department of social science.

To Chapter XXII., &c.—"*Our export trade has already fallen off by an amount much exceeding the entire sum of £135 millions.*"

There is yet another method by which the truth and actual bearing of this matter may be made palpable to the public. In the various States the actual laws adopted follow the theories which governments think right, and it stands to reason that such theories influence the practice, independently of supply and demand. The question then is :

What advantages has England derived from her exclusive gold valuation ?

The mere allegation that we have had the "single" standard is of no statistical value whatever. True, the almost uninterrupted prosperity which lasted until 1872 enabled the gold party to point to this as a result. The prosperity of England was not, however, due to gold, but to the power of manufacture and commerce of the country. France, with its bi-metallic system made even greater advance, Germany and other States under silver valuations did not lag behind ; in fact all nations made good progress. The most characteristic saying respecting this point was uttered by Mr. Disraeli in 1873 (See Chapter XVII.), when he said, "*Our gold standard is not the cause of our commercial prosperity, but a consequence of our commercial prosperity,*" which means, in reality, that we could bear with the gold valuation as a kind of luxury, in spite of certain disadvantages which were then not so visible, but which, since the equilibrium was upset, have come upon us with unerring force.

Now, inasmuch as the decline of our trade during the last five years has shown us that the spread of the gold system has done us great harm, the question should rather be :—

For what purposes has England made these sacrifices ?

As shown in Chapter XVIII. we have in this country, apart from banknotes and copper coins :—

Gold	£135 millions
Silver Coin	18 „
Together	£153 „

The *rôle* which this metallic currency plays in our internal intercourse is but a partial one. In the London Bankers' Clearing House there is a yearly turn over of between £5,000 and £6,000 millions, and the transactions in the Banking world besides, through cheques, bills, accounts, &c., all over the country, probably far exceeds that amount. A great portion of our community makes its payments in cheques or notes. Even so-called legal tender payments in law proceedings are made by Bank of England notes. The movements of larger quantities of gold, for international purposes, are conducted at the Bank of England and by bullion brokers. Our circulating currency, in fact, performs but the task of effecting that portion of our intercourse which remains, when, by means of the above methods, the vast majority of transactions have been settled. And in this more limited office, the amount of currency in use assumes certain definite dimensions dependent upon numbers of population, prices, and other contingencies already alluded to. (See page 18.)

Now, if we in England adopted the bi-metallic system, we might have in circulation, say ;—

Gold	£105 millions.
Silver	48 „
Together	£153 „

and, whether the proportions varied more or less, gold would always be the principal portion. In any case, the commonwealth, in its internal intercourse, could deal with these proportions without involving any loss whatsoever in the amount of currency, and, it may even be asserted, the total amount would increase, and confer benefits upon the circulation. Indeed, if the question of the weight of silver was not undeservedly made so much of, whilst it has never been one of difficulty with nations on an equal footing with ourselves, it seems proper to say that rather than suffer such great losses, all our own currency might be in silver, so *long as it were of the same amount in value as gold.* But this is not asked here; the question being merely whether we should use gold and silver jointly, or not, the former predominating.

It can now be shown that, because we have been so exclusive and obstinate in reference to this matter, we have already lost, within the last eight years, an amount of money, which exceeds the entire amount of our metallic currency two or three times over, as will appear from the following statement :—

In 1872, the total exports of the produce of the United Kingdom amounted to £255,916,000 ; in 1873 to £255,164,000. From thence they steadily declined until, in 1878, they were only £192,804,000. During the two months of this year (1879) they amounted to £27,000,000, which, compared with the results of last year, might indicate that, for the whole of this year, they are not likely to exceed £185,000,000. Although our export trade reached its highest figures in 1872 and 1873, what valid reason was there for its decline, *i.e.*, its rapid and continuous decline for the last six years? Up to 1872 our trade had continually increased, and no cause whatsoever existed to produce a stoppage at the level then gained, still less to produce a decline, unless it were such an extraordinary cause as demonetisation of silver. If our trade had only ceased to increase, the matter would have been serious enough, and worthy of enquiry, but the rapid decline deserves the most weighty consideration. Up to that time, trade had paid us well in monetary profit. Public and industrial enterprises here and abroad yielded fair dividends, or had the usual prospects of doing so. As to over-production, it can certainly not be said that at that time markets were over-stocked, here or abroad; and the whole business of exchanging the products of nature and labour went on smoothly. Indeed, it can be said that a continuous increase of trade was only in accord with the increase of populations, of means of communication, and other civilising influences. The increase of our machinery and productive power is but a moderate percentage, and would have been perfectly justified, for it bears no proportionate relation whatsoever to the decline of trade. Were it not for this extraordinary cause then, a yearly increase of £5 millions in the exports of British goods, an amount less than 2 per cent., would seem to be quite a moderate estimate. It would not be out of the way to say that the export of the produce of the United Kingdom, amounting to £255 millions in 1872, instead of having declined to £192 millions, might now, in 1878, have been £285 millions.

Comparing then, this, possible increase since 1872 with the actual returns, we obtain the following :—

EXPORTS OF BRITISH GOODS.

	Possible totals.	Actual returns.
1873	£260,000,000	£255,164,000
1874	265,000,000	239,558,000
1875	270,000,000	233,494,000
1876	275,000,000	209,693,000
1877	280,000,000	198,893,000
1878	285,000,000	192,804,000
1879	290,000,000	185,000,000 (estimated)
	£1,925,000,000	£1,505,606,000

thus showing a loss of £420 millions in purchasing power.

But it may be said : this is, after all, an assumption; and therefore, not calculating upon this reasonable increase, let it be assumed that our trade should have merely stopped at the level attained in 1872, when the following statement will apply :—

	Actual returns.	Decline since 1872.
1872	£255,961,000	—
1873	255,164,000	£797,000
1874	239,558,000	16,403,000
1875	233,494,000	21,467,000
1876	200,639,000	55,322,000
1877	198,893,000	57,068,000
1878	192,804,000	63,157,000

an actual loss already suffered on exports only of £214,214,000

There are people endeavouring to console the British public by saying that although our export trade has fallen off in value, yet the quantities have not declined in the same measure. But the accounts submitted show, at all events, that in regard to the export of the produce of the United Kingdom *we have lost so much purchasing power*, be it for the acquisition of commodities or of *gold and silver*.

In addition to this loss, what are the other losses and drawbacks involved?

The loss by the Indian Government on exchanges may now amount to about £3,000,000 per annum. The losses on private incomes in rupees are serious to individuals, but perhaps less important on the whole. But those of the Indian Banks and other institutions whose assets are in India, and those of merchants trading with the East, during the last five years and for time to come, involve many millions. What are the losses of bankers and merchants, who have traded in connection with all the other countries on the silver basis? The losses suffered by our manufacturers throughout the country in capital, and the losses borne by the many thousands of our unemployed working population are lamentable, and finally the farmer, the landowner, and even the holders of some kinds of fixed income, are beginning to become involved in the decline.

The losses which this country has suffered by the default of Turkey, Peru, and other bankrupt nations, must be considered apart from the general losses spoken of above. But, nevertheless, it may be pointed out that the severity and rapidity of these collapses was intensified by the unusual depression of trade brought on with such suddenness and violence in consequence of the demonetisation of silver. Even if this is not admitted, it will hardly be denied that the destruction of the credit of Turkey and the other defaulting States would have been more gradual and less ruinous to individuals, had the prosperity which marked the previous commercial history of the century not been so rudely interrupted.

Bearing in mind, moreover, that in the second account furnished above, the present year is not included, and that unless the remonetisation of silver is resolved upon, commerce will get still worse, it is impossible to fix upon the hundreds of millions which this country has actually lost, and may yet be losing, because the advocates of the gold valuation will insist upon England's using a gold currency instead of one of the same value in gold and silver combined. It is, therefore, perhaps not too much to say, that the whole losses already suffered on account of a false currency theory, even now exceed double the entire value of our currency. In Chapter XVI., when speaking of the doctrines of the gold valuation as requiring the abolition of one of the factors, viz., silver, upon which the business of the world has been dependent, this remark is used :—" Doctrines implying such fatalism and fanaticism, and entailing such sacrifices, cannot be well founded, and require revision." The statements and reflections here submitted may again illustrate this necessity.

To Chapters XVI., XVIII. and XX.—" *In either case the Bank of England would be able to use her right of holding a certain proportion of silver in her issue department.*"

Clause 3 of the Bank of England Act is worded as follows :—

And whereas it is necessary to limit the amount of silver bullion on which it shall be lawful for the issue department of the Bank of England to issue Bank of England notes ; be it therefore enacted, that it shall not be lawful for the Bank of England to retain in the issue department of the said Bank at any one time an amount of silver bullion exceeding one-fourth part of the gold coin and bullion at such time held by the Bank of England in the issue department.

In his speech of the 20th May, 1844, Sir Robert Peel said :—

The reasons in favour of permitting the issue of silver with such consent are these :—The facility of exporting silver in preference to gold, when such export is expedient, is the true remedy against the inconvenience of our standard differing from that of other countries; and unless the circulation department is allowed to issue against silver, that inconvenience might occasionally be severely felt.   So long as a silver standard is not recognised and silver coin is used only as tokens under 40s., no quantity of silver likely to be in the Bank can affect the standard value of the gold sovereign : but the sale of that silver may save useless coining of sovereigns, and answer the same purpose.   Silver generally arrives from America, and latterly from China, in large amounts, and at pretty regular periods.   If the Bank is restricted from purchasing that silver, it will always be bought by merchants, who will export it immediately, the principal demand being for the Continent.   No capitalist will find it to his advantage to hold it, the variations in price seldom, if ever, compensating him for the loss of interest.   When the exchange is low, and the price of silver high, this export acts advantageously in liquidation of payments due to foreign countries ; but when the exchange is high and silver low, the silver will sell at a lower price than if the Bank were allowed to buy it, and it will be exported solely for the purpose of bringing back gold, the expense of the export of the silver and the import of the gold being an actual loss on the transaction. The practice of the Bank has been to buy bar silver at 4s. 11½d., and dollars at 4s. 9½d., which at the French mint prices is equal to buying gold at 77s. 9d.   When the exchanges have fallen, and there has been a demand for remittances to the Continent, the Bank has sold the silver, and such sale has answered all the purposes of gold, has left a small profit to the Bank, and saved the expense of exchanging silver for gold.   An unnecessary export of silver, that is, an export when it is not required to rectify the exchanges, causes a momentary rise in the exchange, which again falls back to its original rate, so soon as the operation is ended.   This momentary rise in the exchange, so long as it lasts, is prejudicial to all parties who may have to draw bills upon the Continent in payment for goods and other exports.   A stock of silver in the Bank is convenient to our trade, particularly with India and China   Merchants often require that metal as a remittance, and would have to send to the Continent for it at a greater expense, if they did not find a supply at the Bank.   But if the Bank is absolutely restricted from the issue of notes upon silver, the stock of silver retained by the Bank will be a very limited one, as it will not answer the purpose of the Bank to purchase silver and hold it as a part of its assets in the banking department.   For these reasons, I am inclined to propose that the Bank shall have the power of issuing notes on the deposits of silver.   There should, I think, be a limit to the extent to which this issue shall be allowed.   If we provide that the amount of silver on which issues may take place shall not exceed one-fourth of the amount of gold—(for instance, if there be four millions issued upon gold, permitting an issue upon silver to the extent of one million)—we shall probably insure the maintenance of such a stock of silver as may give facilities for rectifying the exchanging and supplying the demands of commerce, and incur no risk of infringing upon that principle which will impose a positive obligation upon the Bank to receive gold in exchange for notes, and to pay notes in gold coin on demand.

The coincidence of what is here proposed with Sir R. Peel's views of the law is noteworthy.   For the first few years under the new Act the Bank thus held a certain proportion of silver bullion, but then, very wisely, abandoned the practice.   For it is quite evident that under such a curiously worded restriction in the clause above quoted, the practice was not easy.   Sir R. Peel, no doubt, imagined that under the more regular state of the level of bullion, which he hoped for, this proviso would leave some kind of margin ; but, since, for reasons which need not be discussed here, the amount of bullion in the issue began to vary more than before, the Bank was unable to act upon it, even were the varying price of silver no consideration.   If, however, the clause had stipulated for, say "one-fourth of the circulation," instead "of the amount of gold," it would have been practicable.   In any case the clause forms an integral part of the law, and the item "silver bullion" still appears in the weekly schedule.   Now if the proposal made here, viz., that England should coin a 4s. piece under the restricted tender, be adopted, and the clause be altered so as to refer also to such coin in addition to silver bullion, the Bank of England might be able to hold a moderate stock of these pieces for Indian demand.   The State would provide these pieces, without the Bank being called upon to purchase silver bullion at a fixed price, such as the £3 17s. 9d. now paid for the ounce of standard gold.   Nevertheless, the Bank would then be able to contribute its quota to the maintenance of silver.

In the event of the necessity of the adoption of full bi-metallism, however, the Bank would be placed in a different position; a change of great importance would have to be made in her action.   The Bank is so essential a factor in our currency system, her work and organisation in regard to the good order of gold and silver coins being so perfect, that the mere "ex cathedra" command to do this or that, must be subjected to careful consideration. In front stands the question: "Shall the Bank of England pay a fixed price for silver as it does for gold?" If the 4s. piece be adopted, on the basis of 350·625 grains of fine silver, the ounce of the standard silver would be worth 60·78 pence, and making an allowance on the same principle as that for gold of one and a half pence per ounce, the purchasing price of silver might be a fraction less than this assumed standard price. It is said that the obligation of the Bank to pay £3 17s. 9d. for gold is a cardinal principle of the law, but it may be maintained that the real cardinal principle is, that the Mint of this country coins gold at the fixed rate. For it is now well known that the so-called free coinage of gold by the Mint is not a practical reality, that the charge of 1½d. per ounce which the Bank makes for the surrender of notes against bullion, together with other incidents of the business, amount to quite as much as the direct coinage charge made by other Mints,* and that the state or chief issuing banks of other countries are always ready to buy bullion with notes on the same day. Now, if bi-metallism is adopted here in England, the Bank would have to treat silver upon a footing similar to gold. It may, therefore, be still a question whether it is absolutely requisite that the Bank should be compelled to pay an invariably fixed rate for either metal; whether, in fact, it should not have the same liberty which it has now in selling bullion at whatever rate it likes. Those acquainted with the business are fully aware that this liberty to buy and sell cannot range to fancy prices, that it is a mere question of fractions of pence. If the Bank offered too low a price, the importer would go to the Mint and wait; if she held bullion too high for sale, the exporter would take from the circulating coinage; so that there are natural limits in the nature of the business, which compel the Bank and the Mint to act reasonably in these matters. The cardinal principle supposed to lie in the fixed price paid by the Bank is nothing more than this natural understanding, and it holds good in both buying and selling. The Bank might still pay the present price for gold, but why should it not have the right to pay, say, a penny more per ounce for gold if it chose to do so? To the ordinary individual such trifles would seem of no importance, but for hundreds of thousands of pounds they have an attractive or repellant effect, as the liberty to deal may be used, within these narrow limits. The Bank might accordingly use this liberty so as to prevent an undue accumulation of one metal over another, in her own coffers; and the plain justification for this should be the real and assumed capacity of the Mint to coin a certain quantity of pieces, of either gold or silver, to be determined upon fair and reasonable grounds, per day. But it may finally be remarked that in all probability these precautions need rarely, if ever, be exercised. For under the international agreement, as said before, the distribution of the precious metals will settle itself in a natural way; so that this country, for instance, need not fear an undue accumulation of silver, and any momentary redundancy would speedily be reduced by export. The Bank of England is an institution which does not seek a profit in the small differences on bullion; and the correct, as well as the beneficent action which depends on the price of bullion,

---

* "The Question of Seignorage or Charge for Coining." Effingham Wilson, Royal Exchange, 1868.

59

might well be left to the wisdom of its directors. It is more than likely that under their hands the regularity so desirable would be most effectually secured. The Bank of France, for instance, is not bound by law to purchase or sell either gold or silver, but she buys at a rate so close to the Mint price that she makes no profit at all, in fact, at the so-called tariff prices; she is right in doing this, and, on the whole, she keeps the most regular stock of bullion.

This subject of regularity in the stock of bullion covering a note issue has some connection with the rates of interest, and with panics. There are many people who, among other circumstances tending towards such panics, include the fact that we in England are too exclusive in regard to gold, that if we also used silver we should not only enhance our trade, but should have two materials to fall back upon. It may fairly be maintained that under the concurrent use of silver with gold, the Bank of England would have a more ample and regular stock of bullion. But in order that the full meaning of this suggestion may be impressed on the mind of the inquirer, it is above all necessary that the wisdom and the strict validity of a monetary system in which both gold and silver are used, should be freely recognised. Held in the form of bullion for the purpose of security against a bank-note issue, silver requires only the same law as gold; and this, by itself, makes the question of its proper remonetisation important, for it is one independent of the more or less secondary arguments used against that metal. If our Government sees the need for action in this crisis, it may fairly be assumed that the Bank of England will fully respond to this need.

At an international conference on the whole matter, the subject of the charge for the coining of gold and silver full legal tender pieces would have to be considered, and it may be suggested that the liberal method which England has initiated as regards gold coining, might be adopted as the basis for a most moderate scale of charges, founded solely on the strict working cost of the process of converting bullion into coin.

To Chapters II., IV., V., VII., IX., and XVIII.—*The Subsidiary Silver Coinage, its origin in Germany, and its extension in England to all Silver Coins.*

It has been explained before that the principle of subsidiary coinage can be adopted within certain limits without involving any danger or inconvenience. The copper coins, under the restriction of tender to 12 pieces for any single payment, thus rest on a distinct basis, and can be maintained as tokens; but, in considering the two precious metals, the matter stands on a different ground. The usual conception that gold or silver coins derive their value from their true contents in metal, has always been acted upon in former times by the governments, and, except in the case of certain experiments and the acts of tyrannical rulers, all silver coins to the lowest denomination were of full value. The first notable break in this rule appears to have been made by the Germans a century ago. They commenced to issue a fractional coinage, of which the following gives the types :—

Names of Coins.	Proportionate Contents in Silver and Copper.		Nominal Value in English Pence.	Nominal Value in Germany.	Real Silver Value in Germany.
1 Kreuzer	156	844	$\frac{1}{3}$ penny	1 Kreuzer	$\frac{3}{4}$ Kreuzer
3 ,,	333	667	1 ,,	3 ,,	$2\frac{3}{4}$,,
6 ,,	333	667	2 ,,	6 ,,	$5\frac{1}{2}$,,
$\frac{1}{2}$ Groschen	220	780	$\frac{3}{5}$ths,,	6 Pfennige	$3\frac{1}{8}$ Pfennige
1 ,,	220	780	$1\frac{1}{5}$,,	12 ,,	$6\frac{1}{4}$,,
$2\frac{1}{2}$,,	375	625	3 ,,	30 ,,	$26\frac{1}{2}$,,

It will be seen from the metallic proportions shown here that these inferior German coins were really copper coins, but on being "blanched" at the Mint by acids, they bore the appearance of shining silver, the coating of silver wearing off after a while, when the reddish tint would appear. Nevertheless, their intrinsic value, taking into account the copper, was not so inferior in the pieces of the threepenny type. The value of silver being upheld by the coinage of full metallic money and the state receiving the subsidiary pieces in payment at Government offices for taxes or otherwise, a copious issue of these coins could take place for the purposes of internal intercourse. The percentage of these pieces to the general circulation did not exceed 3 per cent., for as all the coins above the value of three English pence were made of full metallic contents, no restrictions being placed on the coining and tender of the larger pieces, there was always a good supply of silver money. In other states, such as France, Russia, &c., the entire silver coinage was "honest" money until 1867.

But when in England in 1816, the *whole of the silver coinage was debased*, an entirely new and untried feature was introduced. Our new silver coinage was made of the same good quality of silver as before, but the quantity of the metal in each coin was reduced. The following table shows what our silver coins are worth in metal at the old mint price of 62 pence, the bi-metallic, or general rate of $60\frac{7}{8}$ pence, and the present temporary price of silver, at, say, 50 pence, compared to the nominal issue rate of 66 pence per ounce :—

British Silver Coins (Fresh from the Mint).

Nominal Value in Circulation.	Real Metallic Value. At old Mint Rate of 62d. per oz.		At Bi-metallic Rate of $60\frac{7}{8}$d. per oz.		At Present Momentary Rate of 50d. per oz.	
	s.	d.	s.	d.	s.	d.
5 shilling pieces	4	8.36	4	7.34	3	9.45
$2\frac{1}{2}$,, ,,	2	4.18	2	3.67	1	9.72
2 ,, ,,	1	10.55	1	10.14	1	6.18
1 ,, ,,	0	11.27	0	11.07	0	9.09
6 pence ,,	0	5.63	0	5.53	0	4.54
3 pence ,,	0	2.81	0	2.76	0	2.27

This shows that, even compared with our old coinage rate of 62 pence, which was too high, our silver coins since 1816 had been reduced in weight, and, taking the bi-metallic rate and the present price of silver, the difference is still greater.

The English sterling silver coins therefore are not pieces of full metallic value, such as the majority of the people have believed them to be, above the coins of all other nations. In former times tampering with the coinage, *i.e.*, its debasement, led to rebellion and misery. Now as rebellion on this account has not taken place in England, are we therefore to suppose that this inferior and dishonest coinage, as this excessive extension of " token " to *all* Silver coins of a State might be called, makes no difference ? The term dishonest is not used here for the purpose of exciting such rebellious feeling, for the law and its motives were clearly expressed at the time, but to indicate that, somehow, this debasement must have an evil effect in some direction or other. This *effect lies in the extreme limitation of the silver coinage* in use.

It has before been shown that the Government alone issues the silver coinage, that its tender is restricted to 40 shillings ; that the State itself does not take it, excepting under the same limit, and that it is debased to prevent its export. The effect of these restrictions is that only a small quantity can be kept in use, and however strong the demand may be, it can only be responded to in a roundabout way, so that the greater part of its force is lost before it can be satisfied, if under the whole aspect of the matter the term satisfaction could at all apply. That under these conditions there must now and then seem to be a surplus of silver, heaped in banks as useless money, is but natural, and this increases the difficulty of establishing an equilibrium between demand and supply.

It is certain that our legislators of 1816 did not contemplate this strict limitation. They no doubt thought that less silver would be used in England than before ; but that their experiment should result in so slender an amount being retained was not in their minds.

The following statement will show the Silver Coinage of the United Kingdom:—

FROM 1790 to 1815	} £1,634	No active coinage. The amount coined in the 25 years was only Maundy money. The active coinage of silver was resumed in 1816.

1816	£1,805,251		
1817	2,436,277		
1818	576,279		In 1821 the population of the United Kingdom was 21,300,000 ; in 1826 it had reached 22,800,000. Allowing for new silver coin taken to the colonies (say £900,000) the £8 millions remaining would be at the rate of 7s. 6d. per head of population in 1826.
1819	1,267,272		
1820	847,717		
1821	433,686	} £8,991,393	
1822	31,430		
1823	285,271		
1824	282,070		
1825	417,535		
1826	608,605		

1827	£33,019		
1828	16,288		The above proportion of 7s. 6d. per head proved too much, complaints of redundancy arose, and but little was coined. Allowing for exports and other reductions, the population to £8 millions was 25,000,000, or 6s. 4d per head.
1829	108,259		
1830	151	} £191,703	
1831	33,696		
1832	145		
1833	145		

FROM 1834 to the year ending 1878.	} the total issued was	£17,700,000	From 1834 the coinage of silver became more settled, though still irregular at times. During this time also the necessity of recoining worn pieces arose, and, making allowance for their withdrawals, exports to colonies and losses, the total in 1878 was £17 millions in circulation, to a population of 34 millions, or 10s. per head, there being in addition about £1 million held by banks.

The remarkable gap in the coining of silver from 1826 to 1834 demonstrates that the actual results of the strictly enforced limit were not expected in 1816. The rate of 10 shillings per head, which the proportion had reached in the prosperous times of 1870-71, seems to be the outside range for a country like England, where prices are highest. The Germans have adopted this rate for their system, and although it has been said that they may require more, yet the Government has denied that it has any intention of issuing more. Indeed in states where prices are lower than in England the proportion of such coins should be less.

It has here been made a chief point to show that this strict limitation of the silver coin, its conversion into "tokens," brings about the demonetisation of silver. Whether the subsidiary coinage in other states is a little more or less than 10 shillings per head of population is not of much moment, the great mass of surplus silver would not be diminished, the question involved therein is the great *international* one, the cause of England's loss in industry and commerce. It has also been hinted in Chapter IX., p. 20, that the demonetisation of silver threatens the maintenance of the entire silver token coinages *for internal purposes*. But quite apart from these considerations there is a prior point worthy of attention, viz. :—

"*Is it just or expedient that the silver coinage of a country should be forcibly confined within such narrow limits ?* "

This question is all the more pertinent because we in England hold to the doctrine that a free supply of money encourages trade, that a surplus even *creates* the demand. But we apply this only to gold, which we coin free of charge without restriction as to amounts and tender. With silver we follow the *diametrically opposite policy*. Speaking, as is done here, of the "internal " intercourse, it would appear then, that for all business which exceeds 10s. in single transactions there is an abundance of the medium of exchange, but for all under that amount, within the range of silver coins, there is an enforced limitation. The very purpose of money for internal intercourse is that there should not only be adequate divisions and a sufficient number of pieces, but that the element of encouragement should be kept up. It is not sufficient to say, " there seems to be no demand for more silver," and " any man can get a sovereign for 20s. silver," and *vice versa ;* nor does the command " to earn a pound in gold and then get ' change' for it," answer the matter at issue. This matter may fairly be brought forward, without it being supposed that there is any desire to set class against class.

The wealthier strata of society in England not only have at their disposal the banking and clearing system, but the free supply of gold and the use of silver. Including in their ranks all persons who earn 10 shillings a day, they do not form more than one-eighth of the population.* Of the remaining seven-eighths of the population, only a portion are employed in centralised industry, such as manufactures for export, the majority having chiefly to rely on *mutual dealings among themselves*. The latter is, therefore, by far the greater interest. This large section of the population cannot deal effectively in cheques, rarely only in banknotes, only

* Our Income Tax Returns show in the United Kingdom that there were paying in 1874 :—

88,971 Persons on incomes of from £100	to	£200 a year.
72,215	,,	,,	200	,,	400	,,
42,493	,,	,,	400	,,	1,000	,,
11,496	,,	,,	1,000	,,	2,000	,,
6,409	,,	,,	2,000	,,	4,000	,,
2,980	,,	,,	4,000	,,	10,000	,,
1,146	,,	,,	10,000	,,	50,000	,,
97	,,	,,	50,000	,,	and more	,,

224,816 total, above say, 10s. a day.

partially in gold, and chiefly requires the smaller denominations for which silver alone is suitable. These simple facts are beyond dispute.

Unfortunately the economy of this country has been too much guided by our Custom House statistics, as if the life of the labouring classes were solely dependent thereon, and much of our financial policy has been influenced by this kind of international rivalry. The great everyday question of mutual life between the people themselves in its connection with money has been neglected. Whenever the subject has been brought forward, the modern gold school fiercely repudiated enquiry into the justice of the matter. The usual allegation was that : " the system had worked satisfactorily ; there was no demand for more silver ; " " that if there was such demand it would be certain to assert itself," &c., and similar phrases were used to justify the gold policy.

The satisfactory working of our gold valuation was due to its being an essential factor in the general international equilibrium as explained in Chapter V., page 9, but the strength of this country as regards manufactures and international commerce should not be confounded with the question of internal intercourse. Just as a plant may grow in a confined space, and in spite of neglect may somehow live, whereas proper treatment would give it a strong existence, so is there something puzzling in our own internal difficulty of excessive pauperism, which might disappear if the medium of exchange were not unnaturally restricted. The fact that food is obtained by the poor, whether by public or private charity, is proof that as a nation we have, or acquire sufficient, in any case. The poverty is rather owing to the absence of commodities above mere food, which might be produced, or of mutual services which might be rendered, between the lower classes themselves, apart from the exchanges generated by the industry concentrated in factories. But, unless there are a sufficient number of the right kind of means of exchange available in the country, the *ex-cathedrâ* command to the people to work for each other, is useless. The demonstration that there is more demand for silver cannot be made by word of mouth, whether by one spokesman from the people's ranks or by all voices united. Those to whom such an appeal would have to be addressed would probably shout with derision at the barefaced impudence of such an attempt. The only demonstration possible is the silent suffering of millions, with all its accompanying evils of vice and crime. The policy of the governing classes in this matter is all the more foolish, because this is not a case in which one gains and the other loses ; the improvement of the lower classes would strengthen the foundation on which the upper classes rest.

Many readers may concede that there is nothing sentimental in this representation of the matter, that on the contrary, the plain arithmetical ground on which it is based is an intensely real one. The author naturally expects that he will be abused for stating the case in this form, but it is the only practical method of calling attention to its "academical" nature, that is, its connection with the wider question of the scientific and practical problem of the standard of value.

So long as England's prosperity in international commerce lasted, until it gained its highest state in 1872, the anomaly in regard to the subsidiary silver coinage here pointed out, was, to a certain degree, concealed, so to speak, by the general welfare, and kept from coming to the foreground. But now that the aspect of trade seems to show the need of England's greater reliance upon her own interior resources, more consideration ought to be given to it. The extension of the same system to other less favoured nations may produce a much more marked effect. In Germany, for instance, its adoption has already promoted pauperism, and the secret and dangerous social movements there observable are omens of the baneful influence of this wrong. The German Government is obliged to favour protection, both for the purpose of keeping a hold on the gold acquired, and in virtue of the necessity of reserving more labour for the people; thus one disease is engendered by another. Should the nations not come to an understanding on the question, should other countries be forced to adopt the same course, the claims of justice may assert themselves in a manner compared with which all that has been experienced in the history of social uprising will be cast into the shade. We in England can prevent this, by allowing the addition to our silver currency spoken of in Chapters XVIII. and XX., not only for the sake of ourselves, in our international and internal interests, but for that of humanity at large.

To CHAPTER XIV.—"*The Indian Council Drafts are only a different method of settling an account.—The financial position of the Indian Government and people is in a precarious state.*"

It is alleged that the Council bills drawn by England upon the Government of India now interfere with the Indian Exchange, because whilst in the years 1858 and 1860 they amounted to less than £1 million, they have since risen to £12 and £13 millions per annum. The truth of the matter is that *such bills have always been drawn* upon India, even by the old East India Company. The Company, moreover, not only sold Indian merchandize in London, but also received payments here for advances on goods. Bills on London were remitted by the Government, and occasionally gold and silver were sent, and certain payments were made in India for account of the Imperial Government. Railway and other companies paid large sums of money to the Council here for transmission to India. These payments, to a great extent, formerly took the place of drafts, but since the merchandise matters were left to private trade, and the railways taken in hand by the State, they have fallen off. The Indian treasury here also paid off old debts and East India stock, and on the other hand raised fresh loans for India. The Council drafts therefore involve rather another and better method of settling an account, and not a new feature operating against the Indian Exchange.

The following table, computed from the published statement of the India Office, will show this. The *first* column contains the *balances* held in England for India at the end of each financial year.

The *second* column exhibits the aggregate of *other receipts*. They are : sales of commercial assets and payments for advances on goods up to the year 1850; payments in India for account of the Home Government; various other remittances; and moneys received from guaranteed companies. The latter item was very large, amounting to about £50 millions between 1856 and 1870, but since the State has taken the railways in hand, and the traffic receipts are retained in India, the outlay here has exceeded the other payments since 1874.

The *third* column shows the shortcomings from the above payments between 1874 to 1878, and remittances of bullion made by the Council between 1857 to 1862.

The *fourth* column shows the Home and Indian Loans, &c., redeemed here from time to time. This and the third column are printed in italics to show that they stand on the credit side of the account.

The *fifth* column shows the fresh loans in England for Indian account.

The *sixth* column the bills drawn upon India to make up the balance required.

The *seventh* column the rate of exchange at which they were drawn.

TABLE SHOWING THE AMOUNTS OF COUNCIL DRAFTS ON INDIA FROM 1834 TO 1879, AND THE REASON WHY THEY VARIED IN AMONNT IN £ STERLING.

Years.	Balances in London at end of year.	Various receipts as above described.	Short proceeds and *silver shipments by the State.	Loans, &c., redeemed in England.	Loans, &c., raised in England.	Council drafts on India.	Rates of Exchange.
	£	£	£	£	£	£	
1833—34	3,772,901	—	—	—	—	—	—
1834—35	3,625,488	4,679,506	—	*2,213,852*	—	732,804	1 10¾
1835—36	5,405,807	3,103,047	—	—	—	2,045,254	1 10⅝
1836—37	2,737,440	3,764,718	—	*5,318,806*	—	2,042,232	1 10¾
1837—38	4,246,960	2,897,259	—	—	—	1,706,184	1 11
1838—39	2,928,132	2,240,564	—	*2,472,734*	—	2,346,592	1 11⅜
1839—40	2,020,227	968,020	—	—	—	1,439,525	1 11½
1840—41	1,088,299	1,020,363	—	—	—	1,174,450	1 11⅜
1841—42	1,687,561	1,648,866	—	—	168,900	2,589,283	1 10½
1842—43	988,199	1,341,196	—	—	100,000	1,197,438	1 11⅜
1843—44	1,407,791	—	*358,812*	—	—	2,801,731	1 11
1844—45	1,290,787	196,443	—	—	741,947	2,516,951	1 9⅝
1845—46	1,348,494	990,107	—	—	212,801	3,065,709	1 9¾
1846—47	1,069,499	455,993	—	—	152,231	3,097,042	1 10⅜
1847—48	727,755	1,345,647	—	—	778,342	1,541,804	1 10
1848—49	1,344,431	1,844,826	—	*2,277,875*	1,114,190	1,889,195	1 9½
1849—50	2,106,977	1,995,133	—	*479,887*	—	2,935,118	1 10½
1850—51	2,756,460	1,275,683	—	—	—	3,230,458	2 0½
1851—52	2,365,848	342,694	—	—	—	2,777,523	2 0⅜
1852—53	2,210,357	324,187	—	—	—	3,317,122	1 11⅞
1853—54	2,410,280	717,827	—	—	—	3,850,565	2 0⅛
1854—55	4,767,582	2,960,213	—	—	—	3,669,678	1 11⅛
1855—56	3,431,553	2,216,724	—	*352,869*	—	1,484,040	2 0½
1856—57	3,041,944	1,774,529	—	—	—	2,819,711	2 0½
1857—58	4,361,600	3,406,263	*1,091,033**	*800,000*	6,629,622	628,499	2 0⅜
1858—59	2,819,398	5,025,400	*2,348,765**	*653,900*	6,887,114	25,901	—
1859—60	4,196,093	3,820,040	*3,636,082**	*1,953,000*	12,805,530	4,694	—
1860—61	2,653,063	4,437,753	*364,497**	*956,200*	4,664,605	797	—
1861—62	5,733,711	8,134,217	*735,005**	*1,301,600*	4,995,387	1,193,729	1 11½
1862—63	5,248,910	3,730,760	—	*1,756,200*	—	6,641,576	1 11⅜
1863—64	4,596,274	4,845,825	—	*7,968,500*	2,441,000	8,979,521	1 11⅜
1864—65	3,914,891	2,009,206	—	—	—	6,789,473	1 11⅞
1865—66	2,818,760	1,441,931	—	—	882,800	6,998,899	1 11⅝
1866—67	4,098,779	3,859,304	—	—	2,731,901	5,613,746	1 11
1867—68	2,833,009	6,114,144	—	—	1,164,407	4,137,285	1 11½
1868—69	3,025,981	8,614,644	—	*502,500*	1,534,140	3,705,741	1 11⅜
1869—70	2,892,483	3,356,907	—	*501,300*	4,039,412	6,980,122	1 11¼
1870—71	3,305,972	3,069,601	—	—	2,423,856	8,443,509	1 10⅜
1871—72	2,821,091	1,278,187	—	—	1,413,406	10,310,339	1 11⅞
1872—73	2,998,444	69,976	—	—	—	13,939,095	1 10¾
1873—74	2,013,637	224,901	—	*1,019,000*	1,037,458	13,285,678	1 10⅜
1874—75	2,796,370	—	*649,078*	—	5,070,839	10,841,615	1 10½
1875—76	919,899	—	*1,115,785*	—	1,206,299	12,389,613	1 9⅜
1876—77	2,713,967	—	*1,421,528*	*500,000*	6,216,168	12,695,800	1 8½
1877—78	1,076,657	—	*206,221*	—	4,339,141	10,134,455	1 8¾
1878—79 [Estimated.]	1,281,457	990,600	—	*2,389,500*	3,014,600	12,200,000	1 7½

This table speaks for itself. It shows that from 1859 to 1861 there was no occasion for Council drafts, because of the loans raised here. In the year 1861-62, for instance, there were :—

Balance from last year ...		£5,733,711
Receipts from other sources ...		8,134,127
Loan raised in England ...		4,995,387
Council drafts		1,193,729
Together		**£20,056,954**
Less silver sent by the Council to India ...	£735,005	
Loans redeemed	1,301,600	
		2,036,605
To debit of the home council		£18,020,349

Comparing this with the returns of the year 1877-78 there were :—

Balance of last year	£1,076,657
Receipts from other sources (none)	—
Loans raised in England ...	4,339,500
Council drafts	10,134,455
Together	**£15,540,612**
Less short receipts of previous accounts	206,221
To the debit of the home council ...	£15,334,391

Now all business people will admit that it makes no difference in the exchange whether the above £8,134,127 in 1861 were received here by remittance or were drawn for, yet the exchange in the first case was 1s. 11$\frac{7}{8}$d., and in 1877 stood at 1s. 8$\frac{3}{4}$d. The resumption of the drafts, their increase as such, is thereby explained, and it will be seen that it is a mistake to ascribe India's troubles to them, or to their effect on the exchange.

Great misapprehension seems to exist as to the strain upon India's resources through the present outlay on its behalf in England as compared with previous times. Under the administration of the old Company, officials and other persons carried away many a fortune to England by way of annual drawbacks on India's wealth. Under the present Imperial Government the country is ruled with more efficiency. The improvement in railways and public works, the increase of trade and revenue, are illustrated by the following table :—

COMPARATIVE STATISTICS OF INDIA IN PERIODS.
In £ Sterling and Decimals (00,000 omitted).

	IMPORTS OF GOODS.	EXPORTS OF GOODS.	TOTAL REVENUE.	STATE DEBTS.	RAILWAY MILES.
1843	£7,6	£13,6	£22,6	£35,8	—
1853	10,1	20,5	28,6	40,7	—
1863	22,6	47,9	45,2	96,8	2,335
1873	31,9	55,3	50,2	105,5	5,370
1878*	41,5	65,2	58,6	134,6	7,324

It may be said that an enhanced outlay in England for India at the present time is more justified than formerly, and of the total expenditure in England, over eleven millions are for the payment of interest on loans.

That at this moment the finances of India, and the condition of its internal and international trade, are in a precarious position, cannot be denied. And this is due

---

* It must be noticed that in the official returns furnished by the Indian Government the conversion of rupees into £ is made at 2s., a rate of valuation which is utterly misleading, considering the actual market rate of exchange.

almost entirely to *the demonetisation of silver in Europe, with the concurrent fall in the Indian Exchange and in the value of the Indian currency.* Were it not for this misfortune, the development of India would have proceeded in the usual way ; and her financial and other difficulties would have been overcome with more ease. The decline in the value of silver causes a loss to India in the exchange of at-present £4 millions. The losses on private and other incomes on the rupee basis are also serious. But neither of these losses are so important as those which are suffered in both the import and export trade of India. The fall in silver adds from 25 to 30 per cent. to the cost of imports, an almost prohibitive duty for English goods, apart from customs dues. The rise in prices of produce at Indian shipping ports is no compensation to the people ; it is but the simultaneous proof of the deterioration of their money. Nor must the statistics of shipping goods be here taken as a guide to the actual trade done. The goods sent from England to India have left heavy losses. The Indian Custom House statements, converted into sterling at 2s. per rupee, are also no reliable guide. The best test is that afforded by the bullion going in or out of the country, and, as will now be shown, *India's capacity to absorb bullion has very greatly fallen off.*

In the *following table the trade of England with India,* from 1864 to 1878, is given, according to our own statistics (correcting our exports by adding 10 per cent. for charges). In the *fifth* column the exports of silver from England are stated. In the *sixth* column, computed from the last statistical abstracts of India, the imports of bullion from all other places excepting from England, after deduction of the bullion exported from India, are given; the three columns between them, therefore represent the amounts of money actually retained in India. In the last column, the loans raised in England, after deducting the loans repaid, are stated. (The loans before 1864 and the use made of them appear in the previous table).

TABLE SHOWING HOW INDIA'S POWER OF RETAINING BULLION HAS BECOME WEAKER SINCE 1872, AND THAT SILVER HAS GONE THERE ON ACCOUNT OF THE LOANS RAISED IN ENGLAND IN £ STERLING.

Year.	England's goods trade with India.			Silver sent from England.	Balance of treasure imported into India from elsewhere, and exported.		Treasure retained in India.	Loans raised in England. Balances after redemption.
	Imports from India.	Exports to India.	Balance.		plus.	minus.		
	£	£	£	£	£	£	£	£
1864	52,295,599	22,829,240	29,473,349	4,610,543	15,409,457	—	20,020,000	—
1865	37,395,452	20,717,510	16,678,942	2,944,899	22,445,101	—	25,390,000	882,800
1866	36,901,997	22,738,450	14,663,547	2,148,286	8,326,714	—	10,475,000	2,731,901
1867	25,487,786	25,131,716	356,070	386,699	9,831,301	—	10,218,000	1,164,407
1868	30,071,871	24,496,373	5,575,448	964,574	12,795,426	—	13,760,000	1,091,640
1869	33,245,442	20,362,133	12,883,307	1,417,062	11,402,938	—	12,910,000	3,538,112
1870	25,090,163	22,103,124	2,987,039	1,736,690	1,483,310	—	3,220,000	2,423,856
1871	30,737,385	20,930,877	9,821,771	2,798,376	7,291,624	—	10,090,000	1,413,406
1872	33,682,156	21,936,487	12,244,670	5,677,775	—	2,414,479	3,263,906	—
1873	29,890,802	24,547,687	5,275,225	2,794,479	1,085,521	—	3,880,000	—
1874	31,198,146	27,978,403	3,220,045	6,683,431	—	163,514	6,519,917	5,070,839
1875	30,137,295	28,154,621	1,982,664	3,231,266	—	131,266	3,100,000	1,206,299
1876	30,025,024	26,044,586	3,980,430	8,229,124	—	819,124	7,410,000	5,716,168
1877	31,224,763	29,290,786	1,943,978	14,313,643	926,357	—	15,240,000	4,339,141
1878	—	—	—	3,257,050	—	—	—	3,014,600

It must be borne in mind that these returns are given at the former full prices
F 2

for gold and silver. These full prices still hold good for gold, as it is imported into and exported from India, the gold imports being about one-third of the total bullion imports. On the other hand, since 1872 silver has fallen from 10 to 25 per cent., of which the above returns take no notice. The balances really remaining in India are therefore far less than the nominal amounts obtained from the figures supplied by the Custom House returns.

But without reference to this, the table shows that since 1872 there has been a great change in the power of India to retain bullion. Heavy losses began to be made in the Indian commerce. The exchange and silver at first did not fall so heavily, but trade became weaker and more losses were incurred. The losses to merchants, manufacturers, and bankers concern them in their private accounts, but the statement plainly shows that India has lost the balance of trade in her favour. True, within the last seven years she has retained £40 millions, of which the £14 in 1877 are due to speculation; but what must be borne in mind especially is that she has incurred fresh loans of £20 millions shown here, her total state indebtedness having increased by nearly £30 millions. *Were it not for these continued loans* and other investments in public works, by which money is sent from here to India, the *import of bullion would have ceased already.*

A valuable hint might be deduced from this position. It is evident that India is on the point of seeing the balance of trade turn against her. It has been proposed lately to raise a fresh loan for her of £10 millions. Now whether this sum or a lesser one be raised, it is clear that the interest thereon will swell the annual sum due to us from India. Should such a loan be actually raised, a small percentage of it might go to India in the form of silver, but the reaction would immediately after set in : the necessity of India remitting money here would cause what may be termed the stage of " delirium " in the position of the silver question.

It would then also become evident that the silver held by the Germans and Americans has no commanding influence on the matter. If India had been supplied by the German and American silver in excess of her usual takings, the decline in the value of her exchange and currency would be accounted for; but she has actually taken less than before. It is therefore quite immaterial whether the surplus stock of silver of other nations exists or not. India suffers from the fact that the European nations decline to use silver as money, and not because they also happen to offer some for sale. This true effect of the demonetisation of silver would be made evident as soon as India herself is no longer able to take, or is placed into the position to pay away, silver. The only possible way to avoid this danger is the remonetisation of silver in the way suggested in these pages and elsewhere. India deserves all the more consideration in this, because, in spite of her poverty she has so faithfully adhered to bullion, like ourselves, and the turn between ruin on the one hand, or greater prosperity than ever on the other, hangs upon so slight a thread as the right decision of human intelligence on the matter here under consideration.

To Chapters V. and VI. *The production of gold and silver, and the amount of metallic money in the world at various ages.*

The history of the production of the precious metals may be divided into four periods :—
The *first* and longest is that from "the earliest times, B.C." to the year 1492, A.D., up to the discovery of America.
The *second* dates from 1493 to 1848, in which the figures given are more reliable.
The *third* period extends from 1849 to 1872—*i.e.* from the opening of the Californian and Australian gold mines.
The *fourth* is that from the demonetisation of silver in 1873 to the present year.

As regards the *first*, the statements on the production of gold and silver from "the beginning of the world" are not reliable. In ancient times no statistics were kept, and even at the present day some difference of opinion exists as to the correctness of the returns. Many economists and writers have occupied themselves with the matter. Among these may be mentioned Jacob, Humboldt, Otreschkoff, Rosweg, and others. The ancients had their Californians in certain parts of the old world, but few of the sites are now known. Jacob and others give some account of European and Asiatic mining districts. Burton has lately given a description of the " Land of Midian." Gold was also found in rivers, as it is still found in the Rhine and other European streams in small quantities. Silver mines existed, and silver was extracted from other ores. The estimates made on the quantity of gold and silver from 4000 B.C. to 1492 A.D. vary much. Some authorities, bearing in mind the time of Croesus, Solomon, the Roman and old Indian Empires, with their fabulous riches, think that the sums must have amounted to between £2000 to £3000 millions for the years in question.

How much of whatever it may have been has been used up or lost ? Now here it may first be expedient to give some idea as to the absorption, by abrasion or otherwise, of the precious metals. Of the consumption *of silver* at the present time some information has been given in Chapter VI. page 12. Of the plate thus made a great deal is again melted down, so that the *actual loss* is confined to the *wearing* of plate, and silver *plating not recoverable.* The consumption of *gold plate* is also modified by the melting down of old pieces or ornaments, but the amount lost annually by gilding is probably larger than that of silver by plating. The total of gold and silver thus used at present for other purposes than money has been estimated at between £6 to £7 millions per annum. Of this a portion goes to swell the stock of jewellery and plate, and making allowance for what is again melted down into bullion the actual abrasion is probably smaller than that on coin. As regards the abrasion of coin erroneous impressions seem to prevail; it is much less than old economists have stated. Several of these estimated the abrasion of coin at from $\frac{1}{2}$ to 1 per cent. per annum. In reality the abrasion on our own gold sovereign is less than one-twentieth per cent., that of our silver coinage about one-fifteenth per cent. per annum. Our

English coinage is rather soft in quality, foreign coins have a harder alloy, so that the entire average of abrasion of coin at one-twentieth per cent. covers the case. The life of a coin may therefore be stated as equal to 2,000 years. The actual abrasion on the present stock of metallic money of £1,400 millions in the world is therefore about £700,000 per annum. Now if in ancient times and the middle ages only one-tenth, or one-fifth of the present annual absolute loss in gilding, plating, abrasion of jewellery, plate and coin, took place, it must nevertheless have amounted to a large aggregate.

The estimates of the amount of money at the end of the fifteenth century differ vastly, from £50 millions to £200 millions, but as they mostly referred to Europe, which at that time was not prosperous, whilst the East was in a comparatively better state, it has since been asserted that

in 1492 the stock of money in gold and silver was—

£180 millions.

Of this a very large portion was in the East—India, Persia, &c., less than one-third being in Europe. The amount in jewellery and plate and in hoards was much larger than that in coin; but it is likely that the East possessed a much larger quantity than can here be fairly stated.

In the *second period*, commencing with the discovery of the New World, the mines of America began to be worked; New Granada and the Brazils chiefly for gold; Mexico, Potosi, Chili, Peru chiefly for silver. The Ural mountains in Russia and Africa also added their produce. Considerable quantities of silver were found in Europe. The production between the years 1493 and 1803 is stated at £480 millions of gold, and £940 millions of silver. The latter thus predominated. Between 1803 and 1848 it is given at £160 millions of gold, and £260 millions of silver, so that

The total production between 1493 to 1848 was—
Gold... ... £640 millions.
Silver ... ... 1,200 ,, .

The figures here given are in general agreement with several authorities, who are perhaps more particular as to precise amounts; but no clear dates can be adduced to settle the differences between them. As regards the amounts of plate and jewellery the same want of accurate statistics prevails. The work of Jacob carries the case to 1834, but in a somewhat partial and incomplete manner.

The statistics of coinages available up to 1848, with due allowance for re-coinings, bullion and exchange operations, and other contingencies, show that :—

the amount of money in the world in 1848 was
Gold ... ... £400 millions.
Silver... ... ... 580 ,,
say a total of £1,000 millions in money.

The *third period* dates from 1849, the discovery of the Californian and Australian gold mines, to 1872. The figures of the production of this period also differ somewhat, but those here given are substantially those furnished to the parliamentary committee in 1876 by Sir Hector Hay, a gentleman who has had the best opportunities of obtaining reliable information. His statement may be checked by the statistics given to the committee by other witnesses.

PRODUCTION OF GOLD AND SILVER IN THE WORLD FROM 1849 TO 1872.

YEAR.	GOLD.	SILVER.	TOTAL.
1849	£5,420,000	£7,800,000	£13,220,000
1850	8,890,000	7,800,000	16,690,000
1851	13,520,000	8,000,000	21,520,000
1852	26,550,000	8,120,000	34,670,000
1853	31,090,000	8,120,000	39,210,000
1854	25,490,000	8,120,000	33,610,000
1855	27,015,000	8,120,000	35,135,000
1856	29,520,000	8,130,000	37,650,000
1857	26,655,000	8,130,000	34,785,000
1858	24,930,000	8,130,000	33,060,000
1859	24,970,000	8,150,000	33,120,000
1860	23,850,000	8,160,000	32,010,000
1861	22,760,000	8,540,000	31,300,000
1862	21,550,000	9,040,000	30,590,000
1863	21,390,000	9,840,000	31,230,000
1864	22,600,000	10,340,000	32,940,000
1865	24,040,000	10,390,000	34,430,000
1866	24,220,000	10,145,000	34,365,000
1867	22,805,000	10,845,000	33,650,000
1868	21,945,000	10,045,000	31,990,000
1869	21,245,000	9,500,000	30,745,000
1870	21,370,000	10,315,000	31,685,000
1871	21,400,000	12,210,000	33,610,000
1872	19,920,000	13,050,000	32,960,000
Total	£533,135,000	£221,040,000	£754,175,000

Of this production £350 millions of gold had gone into money, but as stated in Chapter V., page 10, only £60 to 70 millions of silver, making

The total of money in 1872—

Gold	... ...	£750 millions.
Silver	... ...	650 millions.

The consumption for gold jewellery and gilding was very large, as it would be in prosperous times. Silver was largely hoarded in the East.

The *fourth period* is that commencing with 1873, at which date the demonetisation of silver practically set in. The production was:

YEARS.	GOLD.	SILVER.	TOTAL.
1873	£19,240,000	£17,850,000	£37,090,000
1874	18,150,000	14,300,000	32,450,000
1875	19,500,000	16,100,000	35,600,000

The entire production, then, from 1493 to 1875, may be given as:

Gold	... ...	£1230 millions.
Silver	... ...	1469 ,,

The production in the last three years was:

Years.	Gold.	Silver.	Total.
1876	£19,000,000	£14,800,000	£33,800,000
1877	19,400,000	16,200,000	35,600,000
1878	17,300,000	14,700,000	32,000,000

Allowing for what exists now in jewellery and plate, and taking into account the money left before 1493, as well as the use of silver bars, together with the coinage statistics properly adjusted, the total amount of money at the beginning of 1878 was—

Gold coin and bullion ... ... £830 millions.
Silver coin and bullion... ... ... 710 „

As the reader is aware, the demonetisation of silver concerns the £710 millions of silver, and the future supply of that metal for monetary purposes. On the prospects of the finding of more gold fields and the decline in the yield of gold, Chapter IX., page 19, gives information. Those who are beginning to inquire into this question of the demonetisation of silver naturally wish to know how much gold or silver there may be forthcoming. They are actuated by the idea that some compensation would be afforded by more gold or in some other way. In reality it is not of much moment whether either gold or silver are produced in a lesser or greater ratio, excepting that the latter would be the greater benefit. The principal point here is that one of the two metals is to be *repudiated by law.* Of the £710 millions of silver in 1877, Germany and other States have actually demonetised no more than about £60 millions. A part of this has been transferred to other countries, and incorporated with their coinage, another part has been sold as bars; the great mass of silver left in other States is yet in use.

It is expedient here to give the estimates of the precious metals lately made by Dr. Soetbeer, of Goettingen, in Germany. Dr. Soetbeer sums up in Kilogrammes at the full Mint value the production of silver and gold from 1493 to 1875.

Country.	Silver.	Gold.
	Kilogrammes.	Kilogrammes.
Germany	7,904,910	——
Austro-Hungary	7,770,130	460,650
Other European States	7,382,000	——
Russia...	2,428,940	1,033,655
Africa	——	731,600
Mexico	76,205,400	265,040
New Granada...	——	1,214,500
Peru	31,222,000	165,500
Bolivia	37,717,600	294,000
Chili	2,609,000	263,600
Brazil	——	1,037,050
United States...	5,271,500	2,026,100
Australia	——	1,812,000
Various	2,000,000	151,600
Total ...	180,511,485	9,453,345

Value at the prices of pure metal according to Dr. Soetbeer.

Silver ... ... 32,492 millions marks, or £1,592 millions.
Gold... ... ... 26,375 ,, ,, 1,293 ,,

It will be seen that these figures are in excess of those given above. Dr. Soetbeer hints that Sir Hector Hay has underrated the production of silver from other parts than America. It is not unlikely that Dr. Soetbeer has succeeded in obtaining more elaborate accounts of the mines of Germany, Russia, and the interior of Europe than Sir Hector Hay ventured to give. But the difference thus made by Dr. Soetbeer's own figures, does not account for more than an unimportant sum. Sir Hector Hay is the leading partner of a firm of bullion brokers in London of more than a century's existence. There are only three other firms in the business besides his own; the bullion passes through the hands of these houses for verification, and all that goes on here and elsewhere in mining and shipping is familiar to him and others. It is a great question whether elsewhere than here more reliable information can be obtained as to the qualities of bullion arriving from and going to all parts, as to "refining," and the actual "turn out" of the produce of the mines. Dr. Soetbeer, in taking the value of the kilogrammes of gold and silver at the rates of pure metal, has laid himself open to a range of error in his estimates which may affect his figures from 20 per cent. downwards. The tendency to overrate the production of silver for the purpose of showing the "enormous" increase, is only rivalled by the wish to show that there is a "sufficiency" of gold. Dr. Soetbeer gives the production of gold during the five years 1871-75 at the average of 170,675 kilogrammes per annum, or of the total value of about £116,800,000 for the five years. Now, Tooke and Newmarch, and the *Economist*, state the amount at £101,540,000, and Sir Hector Hay at £98,200,000. Why Dr. Soetbeer should differ by £15 to 17 millions, or £3 to 3¼ millions per annum from these authorities and others which may be named, is not easy to see. It is not contemplated here to charge Dr. Soetbeer with any intention to misrepresent the matter, for he is no doubt actuated by good faith, but further on a peculiarity in his method of treating the whole question will be pointed out.

To Chapters V., VI., XVI.—" *The prices of gold and silver in foreign countries, after making allowance for charges of conveyance and mintage either way, corresponded, in their respective measures for weight and coinage, with the price of £3 17s. 10½d. per ounce of gold, and the average rate of about 60⅞d. for standard silver in England.*"

The difficulty of recognising the possibility of maintaining a fixed value by law between gold and silver remains a stumbling block with many people. A good example of this is contained in the *Standard* of the 7th April, 1879. In a leading article, wherein the writer places the principal facts as affecting the interests of England fairly before the public, he nevertheless says :—

"Gold and silver will continue to fluctuate in value, not only in themselves, but relatively to each other, and no legislative rule can be laid down which shall render their position immutable, or which shall keep the two metals running on parallel lines."

The article concludes with the hint that the bi-metallic suggestions involve "*the violation of economic rules.*" This customary saying amounts to "it cannot be," or "it must not be done," and it is so obstinately and constantly asserted, that even if proof to the contrary were given by the experience of centuries, the believers in this kind of logic would shake their heads and insist at least upon saying "it should not be so." For they may say "we have *abundant practical proof* that silver varies in value, for whilst *in London the price of gold remains steady,* the *price of silver is continually changing,* even before the demonetisation of the metal set in, during the 50 years before 1872, these variations in price were marked."

The prevailing custom, therefore, is to compare the London fixed Bank price for gold at £3 17s. 10½d. with the varying market price for silver. Prices for silver and the relative proportions of value between gold and silver are expressed in some such method as this :—

SILVER (per standard ounce).			PROPORTION BETWEEN GOLD AND SILVER.
59	pence	=	1 to 15.98
59½	,,	=	1 ,, 15.85
60	,,	=	1 ,, 15.72
60½	,,	=	1 ,, 15.59
61	,,	=	1 ,, 15.46
61½	,,	=	1 ,, 15.33
62	,,	=	1 ,, 15.21
62½	,,	=	1 ,, 15.08

and so on, through all small fractions, reduced to fine decimals. Some writers go so far as even to give the "averages" at such periods as please them best. They then think that they have furnished minute and conclusive scientific proof of the variation inherent in the matter of "two" standards. Inasmuch as the main argument in favour of the "single" standard is founded on this way of stating the case, may true economists and practical business men now listen to what is the real truth !

It is true that gold here in England has had a fixed mint price, and silver has varied in the London market. Per contra, in other countries, silver has had the position which gold has here, and in the bi-metallic States both metals stood on an equal footing. This ought to be sufficient to show that any reference to the London prices of silver must be quite one-sided, but it may here at once be stated, paradoxical as it may appear, *that the variations in the price of silver in London, furnish the best proof of the maintenance for the last two centuries of the proportion of* 1 *to* 15½ *between gold and silver.*

The general prices of the precious metals depend chiefly upon international trade. The factors which determine the actual movements from one country to another, the so-called shipping points, are: firstly, the *Mint or Bank-prices* in each country; secondly, the *rates of exchange* and the *rate of interest* connected therewith; and thirdly, the *charges of freight,* insurance, and mintage to be incurred, in *either direction.* The latter are unavoidable and mechanical causes; and in order to overcome them, either the exchanges must vary, or the price of the metal itself must be modified. In a country where one metal is at a supposed fixed price, the exchange varies when that metal is in question; for the other metal the exchange requires no direct variations, for the variable price answers the same purpose. As far as corresponding "costs" of these operations against "commodities," or in "general trade," are concerned, it is perfectly immaterial whether the exchange or the price of the metal varies, or whether both together vary simultaneously and proportionately. From this it follows, *primâ facie*, that the fixed proportion between the two metals is also a reality, and has been so throughout, until 1872.

It is altogether an error to suppose that gold in England or elsewhere has that mathematical fixed character on which the quasi-mathematical axiom as to its being " measure " is founded. In the first place, it has two prices. The Bank buys at £3 17s. 9d. per ounce, and sells at an advance of 1½ to 2 pence thereon, having the right to ask still more. In the metallic contents of the current coins themselves the law allows a deliberate divergence of more than ½ per cent., and if double as much were allowed, the power of legislation could so be asserted. In Australia, if bar gold is bought for London, it is not worth more than £3 16s. 2d. per ounce, on account of the charges of shipment of say 2 per cent. ; whilst when coined Australian sovereigns are sent, it is the exchange which diverges by so much. If gold is sent from here to a distance, at 2 per cent. cost, the value becomes £3 19s. 6d., whether for British or foreign account. But the most important variations in the relative value of gold take place in connection with the rate of interest. The principal business, internal or international, is carried on by bills of exchange, without which banking would be impossible. Now if at one time the Bank discounts at 2 per cent., and at another at 10 per cent., the difference on a three months' bill is exactly 2 per cent. The Bank might therefore just as well say : we will continue to discount at 2 per cent. per annum, but charge 2 per cent.—*i.e.*, 1s. 7d. per ounce more for gold. And whether bank-notes, coin, or bullion are in question, for internal or international purposes, the effect is the same. It is said that these effects are "somehow" created by phases of " supply and demand," but it is quite clear that they have nothing to do with the supply from mines, or dearer or cheaper gold, but are inherent in the turnover of the present stock. It is evident, then, that gold itself is not an invariable measure, but that it is a factor with the natural capability to vary, and this does not in any way invalidate its position as a means of exchange. Whether this inherent characteristic, quite distinct, 'as will be admitted, from the causes of variations in other commodities, is expressed in exchanges or in the price of the metal, makes no difference, just as little as there is none between saying : 9 times 10 make 90, or 10 times 9 make 90. Therefore, if on account of the exclusiveness or " singleness " of only one metal, such great variations take place in the rates of exchange for international, and the rate of interest for internal, business, it stands to reason that the two metals joined in the same office would give a better average.

Precisely the same rules as the above apply to States where silver is single or legal tender, the main difference being in the name, gold varying there as silver does here. But just as our fixed rate for gold was the point of departure for its price in exchange, so the fixed Continental rates for silver served our purposes. This point, in sterling, is equal to 60·838 pence per ounce, or say 60⅞d. It rested on the fact that in France 3,100 francs were coined out of the kilogramme 900 fine gold, and 200 francs out of the kilogramme 900 fine silver ; comparing our neutral rate of exchange with France therewith (say £1 = fcs. 25·22½), the above price for silver results. This price is that upon which all the silver states, including India, were dependent in their dealings with ourselves, leading to the following London rates for silver for the last 50 years :—

TABLE OF PRICES IN LONDON OF SILVER FROM 1827 TO 1879.

Year.	Lowest.	Highest.	Year.	Lowest.	Highest.	Year.	Lowest.	Highest.
1827 ...	59½	60¼	1845 ...	58⅞	59⅞	1863 ...	61	61¾
1828 ...	59¼	60½	1846 ...	59	60⅛	1864 ...	60⅝	62½
1829 ...	59½	60	1847 ...	58⅞	60⅜	1865 ...	60½	61⅞
1830 ...	59¾	60	1848 ...	58½	60	1866 ...	60⅜	62¼
1831 ...	60	60⅞	1849 ...	59½	60⅛	1867 ...	60$\frac{5}{16}$	61¼
1832 ...	59¾	60¼	1850 ...	59½	61½	1868 ...	60⅛	61⅛
1833 ...	58¾	60	1851 ...	60	61⅝	1869 ...	60	61
1834 ...	59¾	60⅜	1852 ...	59⅞	61⅞	1870 ...	60¼	62
1835 ...	59¼	60	1853 ...	60⅝	62⅜	1871 ...	60$\frac{3}{16}$	60⅞
1836 ...	59⅞	60⅜	1854 ...	60⅞	61⅞	1872 ...	59¼	61⅛
1837 ...	59	60⅜	1855 ...	60	61⅝	Demonetisation.		
1838 ...	59⅜	60⅛	1856 ...	60½	62¼	1873 ...	57⅞	59$\frac{15}{16}$
1839 ...	60	60⅝	1857 ...	61	62⅜	1874 ...	57¼	59½
1840	60⅛	60⅝	1858 ...	60¾	61⅞	1875 ...	55½	57⅝
1841 ...	59¾	60⅝	1859 ...	61¾	62¾	1876 ...	46¾	58½
1842 ...	59⅛	59¾	1860 ...	61¼	62⅜	1877 ...	53¼	58¼
1843 ...	59	59⅝	1861 ...	60⅛	61¾	1878 ...	49½	55¼
1844 ...	59¼	59¾	1862 ...	61	62⅛	1879 ...	49	

This table shows only the highest and lowest prices, but if the total average be taken of the mean prices, up to 1872, before the demonetisation of silver took place, it will be found to correspond with the bi-metallic rate of 60⅞d. pence.

The reasons why these quotations differ from this real and average rate of 60⅞d. are obvious. They depend upon the charges involved; firstly, on the question whether silver arriving here from mines should go to the Continent or to India; secondly, on the necessity of silver from India and the East being sold here for the Continent; thirdly, on the necessity of expressly importing silver from the Continent for shipment to India. In the first case the questions were those: What are the charges of sending silver to France for mintage? What is the exchange on France? Now, before steam came into use bullion was sent by carriage and sailing cutters from Dover or the Thames. The charges were then three and four times as high as at present. Together with the charge for coinage in France and loss of interest on the operation they may have amounted to 3 per cent., accordingly—

If 1 kilogramme of 900 fine silver at the French mint was coined into ...	frs. 200
There were to be deducted charges of freight, insurance, mintage and incidental of	6
Leaving ...	frs. 194

Which, at the exchange of, say frs. 25·22½ gave £7 13s. 10d.

so that the corresponding 31,281 ounces of British standard silver required for the kilogramme of 900 fine silver could be paid for in London at 59 pence per ounce. In recent years, when charges of forwarding were reduced to about ¼ per cent., the account would have stood—

One kilogramme of silver 900 fine at	... 200 frs.
Charges ¼ per cent. and the coinage charge being frs. 1·50.	... 2
	frs. 198

At the exchange of frs. 25·22½ equal to £7 17s.

so that 60¼d. could be paid. It is evident, however, that the difference between 59 and 60¼ pence in the price of silver in London is not due to phases in general supply, but to the alteration in the mechanical charges. The *fixed price* is the frs. 200 per kilogramme *in Paris*, and whether the charges are paid in Paris in francs or in London in shillings make no difference, and whether gold or silver were sent, there would have been no difference whatever, excepting the slightly lower charge of mintage for the former.

The shipping of silver to India takes place upon the same simple principles. It may be expedient here to give an actual transaction to show this—

Invoice of 52 silver bars from London to Calcutta.

Viâ Southampton P. & O. steamers.

52 silver bars, weighing 51,256·5 ounces of various fineness, from B.16½ to B.17½, equal to British standard ounces—55,237·8, at 61¼d			£14,097	2 10

Charges.

Freight 2 per cent. on £14,000...	£280 0 0	
52 boxes, packing, cartage, bills of lading, &c. ...	11 19 6	
Brokerage ⅛ per cent.	17 12 6	
		309 11 11
Insurance on £15,000 at 7s. 6d. and duty ...	... ...	60 0 0
Cost in London		£14,467 3 9

In Calcutta, at the mint, these bars are weighed in tolas, re-melted, and re-weighed, assayed, and after deducting the charge for mintage, usually paid for in a week's time, the result will be as follows :—

Account Sales in Calcutta.

52 silver bars weighing ... ... tolas 136664·2		
After melting ... ... 136634·4		
Of 997 to 994 fine ... ... total value in rupees	rs. 145452	0 0
Loss in melting ... tolas 29.8		
Spillage recovered	16	5 9
	rs. 145468	5 9

Charges.

Landing and conveyance to mint	22 14 0	
	rs. 145445	7 9

Thus giving an exchange of 1s. 11¾d. per rupee.

That is to say, if the shipper in London, after paying the English bill stamp, could sell his draft upon Calcutta, at 8 days, going by the same mail, at 1s. 11⅞d. per rupee, there would be no loss to him. But as a rule shipments of this kind are made for the purchase of exchange in Calcutta on London ; so the rate of interest for the time spent in going out, the time for return of remittance, and, lastly, the discount of the time the bill has to run in England must be added, and taking these items as they stood at the period shortly before the opening of the Suez Canal, at say 8 months, and 5 per cent. ;

either the Calcutta long exchange ought to be 2s. 0⅝d. per rupee,

or the price of silver in London at 59¼ pence, instead of the 61¼d. paid as above.

In former times, when sailing ships had to go round the Cape, freight and insurance were double and treble as high, and the voyages out and back took many months, so that a total of 10 to 15 per cent. of charges for the above shipment were incurred. In recent years, however, since the Suez Canal opened, the freights have been reduced to ½ per cent., and telegraphs enable us to operate from day to day.— The effect all this had on the rate of exchange and on the prices of both silver and gold as they *were actually vaid* has no connection with the general value of the metals.

Unfortunately, ill-informed persons are in the habit of talking of the illegitimate profits of "bullion merchants and brokers." There can be nothing more wrong. Indeed there are no bullion merchants, for bullion cannot be kept in stock. Every merchant or banker can make these shipments; the question only is : Is it better to buy exchange, or to ship bullion? The terms upon which bullion can be bought, shipped and sold, being known, the sender employs a firm of bullion brokers, who arrange the technical matters of the shipment, and for this service a "brokerage" of one-tenth per cent. is a distinct and legitimate item. This bullion business, especially that in the hands of certain large shippers (who for all that are not bullion merchants), is reduced to a a level where profits may be said to have altogether ceased, for it commences already when exchange and shipments are at an infinitesimal difference, or even as yet equal. In truth, it is nothing less than a superior international clearing system, and those who are able to appreciate the plain logic and mathematical certainty of the business will admit that it is an error to talk of undue profits made by those engaged in it.

Referring now to the above list of prices of silver in London it will be noticed that in the period from 1827 to 1849 they stood generally lower than between 1850 to 1872. This is partly due to the previous higher charges, and partly to the fact that whenever the price was lower, silver went to the Continent. During that period, silver came also occasionally from India and China to England, and had to be sold to France, Holland, or other places. The comparative regularity of the prices will show not only the equalising effect of the gold exchange under the bi-metallic systems, but the quietude of the situation generally under the then undisturbed state of equilibrium.

From 1850, however, the price of silver in London rose from $61\frac{1}{2}$d. to even $62\frac{3}{4}$d. in 1859. The fact is that before 1850 the demand for silver for both Europe and India was satisfied by the general supplies from mines. But shortly after the discovery of the new gold fields and the great encouragement of trade all over the world, there arose so strong a demand for Indian goods and for remittance of silver to the East, that the ordinary supply no longer sufficed, and it became necessary to make very heavy shipments of bars and even of the actual coined silver from the continental markets. Accordingly, *silver in France rose to a premium*, as the quotations seem to show, and it is on this account that so many false conceptions are current. The truth is that in the French bullion market, silver was quoted at the old obsolete mint prices (before 1835) of 218.89 francs per kilogramme fine, whereas the full mint rate is 222.22 francs for pure silver, or 200 francs for 900 fine. The premium quoted on the old price, say, of $1\frac{1}{2}$ or 2 per cent. *was therefore not real.* The prices in Paris were, in principle, the same as the full rate of £3 17s. $10\frac{1}{2}$d. or 11d. which the Bank of England charges for gold. Now, if at these full mintage prices silver was shipped to England, the amount would be : —

One kilogramme 900 fine silver at 15 per mille premium (equal to the difference between the old price of 218.89 and 222.12 fine silver ...	frs. 200
Brokerage, shipping, charges, &c.	3
	frs. 203
And the exchange is taken at frs. 25 $12\frac{1}{2}$, as is the case usually when there is a demand for counter remittance to France, the above costs in London	£8 1s. 7d.

so that the corresponding 31.281 oz. could not be sold under 62 pence per ounce.

At times a slight additional premium had to be paid upon the Bank price, the Bank of France exercising the same right as the Bank of England to refuse to sell bullion. Occasionally, also, the continental markets became exhausted of silver bars, and 5-franc pieces had to be taken from the circulation, either to be melted into bars or shipped to India in their coined state. Now just as much as our Bank price for selling bar-gold is, say, £3 17s. 11d. per ounce, whilst the sovereigns in circulation may differ from this full weight by $\frac{1}{4}$ per cent., so is the 5-franc silver piece subject to abrasion, by perhaps more than 1 per cent. Consequently, if French bankers, who had to employ special agents to collect large masses of silver coin from the circulation at some expense, charged 3 or 4 per cent. on the old-fashioned quotations for silver; or a premium of $1\frac{1}{2}$ to 2 per cent. on the nominal value of the coin ; or, finally, according to directions, caused the coin to be melted into bars, with the usual wastage and expense, and then made a price for the British ounce; the price of that ounce at $62\frac{3}{4}$ or 63 pence, or the supposed premiums, all came to the same thing. These fluctuations, it must be again repeated, had no relation to variations in the supply from the mines, being solely caused by dealings in the existing stock. And if India had required gold instead of silver the total effect on the Exchange would have come to a similar result of cost.

As a further specimen of the current prejudice engendered in this matter, a paragraph from an article in the *Manchester Examiner* of the 7th April may be quoted, wherein the writer, " Verax," says :—

In consequence of the gold discoveries, gold became more plentiful, and sank in value relatively to silver as well as to all other exchangeable things. It therefore paid the bullion brokers to take gold to France and exchange it for silver at the fixed rate. The dearer metal left the country, the cheaper metal took its place, and in a few years France was almost emptied of its silver coins.

The statement that " France was almost emptied of silver " is a mistaken assertion. The total sum of silver sent from France was about £40 millions, and there were at least £100 millions left. For the £40. millions, it is true, France received gold in exchange, alongside of the £240 millions of gold which she acquired by her commerce from 1850 to 1870. The axiom—" The one metal gets cheaper, the other dearer, and therefore leaves the country "—does not apply in this case; yet the case of France is currently quoted as the most extreme illustration in its support.

So much pains to show all this in its true light has here been taken, because it is time that a stop should be put to the misrepresentations founded on the London prices of silver. Those who cannot see the plain truth would say that the price of, for instance, 59 pence per ounce shows the proportion of 1 to 15.95, and that of 62 pence 1 to 15.08 between gold and silver, and found the whole of their theory upon these variations. Those who can see what is real here will, on the contrary, come to the conclusion that the London prices are just the best evidence of the stability which has existed between the two metals. It is true that before the discovery of America the proportions differed more, and this will be referred to presently. But for the last two centuries the rate of 1 to 15.5 has been steadily maintained, and it is to be hoped that the principles of true economy will no longer be violated by denying this. For it will be clearly seen that even the London price on which the monometallists rely is, when properly investigated, a complete proof of the validity of bi-metallism.

To CHAPTERS VI. AND XVI.—*The misuse made of the quotations of London Prices for Silver here and abroad.—Dr. Soetbeer's methods of treating the question.—The real facts of the case shown by a comparative table.—Complete proof of the effectiveness of Bi-metallism.*

The constant error of some of our own economists and statesmen (Mr. Goschen included) of taking the London prices of silver as proof of its varying value, is imitated by certain writers abroad. Among these the name of Dr. Soetbeer, the champion of the German gold valuation, stands prominent. In his work on the production of the precious metals alluded to before, when speaking of the variations in the relative value of gold and silver, Dr. Soetbeer almost entirely founds his calculations upon *the quotations of the price of silver in London.* In the " Goettingsche Gelehrte Anzeigen," of the 19th March, 1879, page 373, the following remarks precede a table showing these variations :—

The relative value between gold and silver, from 1687 to 1832, is given in accordance with the bi-weekly business quotations of the Hamburg course of exchange, and from 1833 to 1878 it has been statistically determined by the London bullion brokers in as complete and exact a manner as can be desired, and the assumption does not seem venturesome, that the yearly averages therefrom may be regarded as absolutely conclusive.

The portion of the table from 1641 to 1875 then states the variations of value, 1 gold to—silver, as follows :—

Periods.	Relations of Value.	Periods.	Relations of Value.	Periods.	Relations of Value.
1641 „ 1660	14.50	1741 to 1750	14.93	1811 to 1820	15.51
1661 „ 1680	15.00	1751 „ 1760	14.56	1821 „ 1830	15.80
1681 „ 1700	14.96	1761 „ 1770	14.81	1831 „ 1840	15.75
1701 „ 1710	15.27	1771 „ 1780	14.64	1841 „ 1851	15.83
1711 „ 1720	15.15	1781 „ 1790	14.76	1851 „ 1860	15.36
1721 „ 1730	15.09	1791 „ 1800	15.42	1861 „ 1870	15.48
1731 „ 1740	15.07	1801 „ 1810	15.61	1871 „ 1875	15.95

Now, if it is wrong to base the proof of the existence of variations on London prices, it is still more unsuitable to take Hamburg quotations. That market, with its slower methods and higher charges, was even more subject to departures from the fixed rates ; and necessarily lower than London. Dr. Soetbeer however is so strongly wedded to the London prices that he applies them to diagrams, and to all periods and circumstances indiscriminately, unaware that the foundation upon which he thus relies for his calculation, would prove the very opposite conclusion, if properly used. Were it not for the evil influence which such methods exercise, the economical error could be treated as a joke; unfortunately too much mischief is created by legislation based thereon.

A characteristic example of the disposition of Dr. Soetbeer to make out " variations " is shown by the way in which he lumps the years 1871 to 1875 as under the average of 1 to 15.98. In 1871 the mean price of silver in London was 60¼, in 1875 it was 56½ pence per ounce. In 1873 the German demonetisation commenced, principally under the advice of Dr. Soetbeer himself. Nevertheless he simply states the average of the five years, as if the rate of 1 to 15.95 was only the result of natural causes, and although he makes some reference to the change in Germany, yet his intention appears to be that of pointing to some mysterious force as the cause of the fall of silver.

Is this power the varying supply from mines ? Very few people will hesitate in answering: "Yes! for it is upon the differences in supply that these variations must take place." Indeed the objection urged against the concurrent use of gold and silver is based upon a mathematical theory, which asserts, that as one metal is produced at one time in greater quantity than the other, so it must fall in relative value to that other. *The actual facts utterly contradict this axiom!* Dr. Soetbeer gives the above variations in the relative value between gold and silver in one part of his treatise and in another the variations in the supplies, but he seems to avoid putting them into juxtaposition so as to show the connection between them.

The following table, however, will now exhibit this. It gives the figures submitted by Dr. Soetbeer himself of the production in kilogrammes of gold and silver, and the proportions of relative value from 1621 to 1875. The columns showing the proportions of percentage in value and those of weight are supplied by the writer.

TABLE SHOWING THE PRODUCTIONS OF GOLD AND SILVER, THE PERCENTAGES IN VALUE AND PROPORTION OF WEIGHT, AND THE PRESUMED RELATIVE VALUE* FROM 1621 TO 1875.

Years.	Gold. Kilos. (Dr. Soetbeer.)	Silver. Kilos. (Dr. Soetbeer.)	Percentage in value.	Proportion in Weight.	Relative Value.* (Dr. Soetbeer.)
1621 to 1640	8,300	393,600	25 to 75	1 to 47.4	1 to 14.00
1641 „ 1660	8,770	366,300	27 „ 73	1 „ 41.6	1 „ 14.50
1661 „ 1680	9,260	337,000	30 „ 70	1 „ 36.3	1 „ 15.00
1681 „ 1700	10,765	341,900	33 „ 67	1 „ 31.7	1 „ 14.96
1701 „ 1721	12,820	355,600	36 „ 64	1 „ 27.7	1 „ 15.27
1721 „ 1740	19,080	431,200	41 „ 59	1 „ 22.6	1 „ 15.08
1741 „ 1760	24,610	533,145	42 „ 58	1 „ 21.6	1 „ 14.74
1761 „ 1780	20,705	652,740	33 „ 67	1 „ 31.5	1 „ 14.73
1781 „ 1800	17,790	879,060	24 „ 76	1 „ 49.3	1 „ 15.09
1801 „ 1810	17,778	894,150	24 „ 76	1 „ 50.0	1 „ 15.61
1811 „ 1820	11,445	540,770	25 „ 75	1 „ 47.2	1 „ 15.51
1821 „ 1830	14,216	460,560	33 „ 67	1 „ 32.3	1 „ 15.80
1831 „ 1840	20,289	596,450	35 „ 65	1 „ 29.4	1 „ 15.75
1841 „ 1850	54,759	780,415	52 „ 48	1 „ 14.2	1 „ 15.83
1851 „ 1855	197,515	886,115	78 „ 22	1 „ 4.4	1 „ 15.76
1856 „ 1860	206,058	904,990	78 „ 22	1 „ 4.3	1 „ 15.76
1861 „ 1865	198,207	1,101,150	74 „ 26	1 „ 5.5	1 „ 15.48
1866 „ 1870	191,900	1,339,085	69 „ 31	1 „ 6.9	1 „ 15.48
1871 „ 1875	170,675	1,969,425	57 „ 53	1 „ 11.5	1 „ 15.95

* As shewn in the last chapter, those decimal variations given by Dr. Soetbeer are only due to freight and other charges, the actual rate being firm at 1 to 15.5.

It will be admitted that this table does not in any way bear out the theory that the greater supply of the one metal over another causes its decline in relative value. Were it not for the facts before explained as to the higher charges of forwarding, it would appear that the value of silver from 1620 to 1680 decreased on the increase of the gold production. In 1810 the production of silver was eleven times as high as in 1851 and 1860, and yet no change took place. Throughout the table there are the greatest variations without having caused any effect. Can anything be more conclusive as to the utter fallacy of the supposed "mathematical" principle ?

Many enquirers might now ask why such a table has not been published before ? The fact is that in this controversy there are but few writers. Those in favour of the monometallic system have hitherto contented themselves with *asserting* that the varying supply *must have the effect they suppose*, without *even examining the actual results*. At a meeting of the Statistical Society of the 1st April 1879, Professor Jevons, after using the ordinary platitudes, said : " The value of silver, of course, falls as the ratio of weight given rises." Like Dr. Sootbeor, Mr. Jevons belongs to the class of men who violate the rules of supply and demand by their onesided view respecting them. Unable to realise that at least two-thirds of the demand for the precious metals owes its force to the use of the precious metals as money, for which they are naturally fit, this class of economists despises the plain law of consent upon which this can be upheld. They do this because they have an objection to " law," but at the same time they want to employ the law to suppress silver altogether. Nothing can be more contradictory to the foundation of the very principles of supply and demand. The natural consequence of this weakness is that such a practical investigation as exhibited by the above table proves the false pretence. The table demonstrates that the force of the demand, regulated by legislation, is strong enough to maintain the steady relation of value between gold and silver in spite of the most extreme variations in the supply from mines, and nothing can speak more strongly in favour of the correctness of bi-metallism. The fact that this regularity was so completely upheld, even under the conflict of valuation systems, as described on pages 6 to 10, which resulted in a more or less *accidental* equilibrium, indicates the great strength of the principle of bi-metallism under a better, if not a universal international understanding.

To CHAPTERS V. AND XVI.—*The variations in the relative money value of the precious metals in ancient times and the middle ages.—The rivalry and vagaries of Legislation contrary to the dictates of the laws of supply and demand.—The force of the law nevertheless effective.*

If now from what has been said in the preceding parts it should seem evident to the inquirer that during the two centuries the proportion of 1 to 15·5 has been substantially upheld, the principle upon which that fact rested will now assist in clearing another mystery.

Before 1620 the relative value of gold and silver was in favour of the latter, and certain variations took place which will be shown by the following statement. As regards this the following consideration must be kept in view :—

Firstly, the information regarding the old coinages is imperfect, and does not afford us more than partial data. A great deal depends on surmises, and the uncertainty of obtaining reliable information is illustrated even by what may happen in modern times, for until the year 1854 we were not aware that the Japanese appeared to hold the rate of 1 to 4.5 between gold and silver.

Secondly, the proportions in former times have been determined from records, but the old gold coins were generally made from nearly pure metal, whilst silver was more or less alloyed. In the assays of certain specimens of old coins a great deal of diversity has been found. Japan, again, affords us an example of the unreliability of statements. For although the proportion between gold and silver was stated at 1 to 4.5, it was found afterwards that some of the Japanese gold coins contained but one-third of their weight in gold.

Thirdly, in the olden times it was difficult to reconcile the differences between neighbouring countries. These differences could exist on account of the heavy charges of conveyance. A sum of £1000 in silver weighs about two cwt.; in the passage along bad roads, what with armed escort, with the slow progress, the exactions and dangers from violence, charges amounting to 10 or 20 per cent. were frequently absorbed; not to speak of the return of gold and of interest lost. Even in the middle ages these difficulties existed, and the conveyance of specie from London to Edinburgh involved heavy costs. So we find that between France, England, Germany and other places, differences in rates existed which could not be redressed by the usual power of supply and demand. All that has been said respecting this subject of charges for the time since 1620, applies in much greater measure to the earlier periods.

Fourthly, the governments and tyrants of the old and middle ages were in the habit of exacting heavy so-called seignorages, taking what they pleased off the coin. Silver was the generally prevalent material, and the opportunity to make a profit from it lay nearest. Most of the Governments also took possession of the mines, and treated their yield at their own option. The use of gold checked extreme fluctuations, but the force of death penalties and other restrictions had their effect in spite of the laws of supply and demand. As a rule gold coin was made when and in whatever manner the Sovereign chose, and distinct mint laws were not established until this century.

Fifthly, we have no evidence that the variations were caused by varying supply of the precious metals. Vague hints to that effect, as regards ancient times, have been made, but they are probably as opposed to the facts as those shown in the table on page 81 for the last two centuries.

Period from 1600 b.c. *to* 400 b.c.

Ancient inscriptions and old Persian coins seem to show that the proportions between gold and silver were as 1 to 13·33 down to the year 400 b.c., or for a period of 1200 years. In the same period, however, the Greek coinage of the year 400 b.c. showed the proportion of 1 to 12, the maintenance of this difference being due to the difficulty of exchanging without heavy charges. The concurrent existence of the divergency at the same moment between two or more nations shows conclusively that the human practice, or the law, as it was, enjoyed an independent influence.

Period from 400 b.c. *to* 400 a.d.

In the Greek and Roman times the proportion was 1 to 12, in Egypt the rate of 12·50 prevailed in 323 b.c., and during the 800 years here comprised the proportions in Rome varied under different Governments, being successively 11·94, —11·80,—11·97,—12,—12·17,—&c. That is to say, these several variations were chiefly due to the uncertainty of the then backward art of assaying and refining, and to attempts at slight debasements in the coinages. The differences in the fine decimal fractions indicated are no more than the divergencies that arise even in this day, when the so-called "remedies" and allowances for current weights are taken into account. In 218 b.c., an extreme attempt in Rome to make gold worth 17·14 speedily failed; a like proceeding in 100 b.c. in favour of a rate of 1 to 8, and another in 312 a.d., for 1 to 14·40 had a similar fate; the ruling proportion being throughout the rate of 1 to 12.

84

Period from 400 *to* 1500, A.D.

During these comparatively dark times in the history of money, there were the usual attempts to tamper with the coinages, but the extreme fluctuations do not seem to have been very great. Gold was made current by edicts and proclamations, and the rate was fairly maintained until the middle of the 14th century, when variations of from 11.20 to 12.0 occurred in different countries. None of these had any connection with varying supply, but are solely due to the wills of the governments. The ruling rate remained at 1 to 12.

Period from 1500, A.D., *i.e., since the discovery of America.*

The great acquisition of treasure arising from the discovery of America opens the period of struggle during which the previous rate of 1 to 12 has been changed to 1 to 15.5, as it prevailed until 1872.

The first natural suggestion is again that this change is due to the greater supply of silver. For the purpose of showing this popular error, and by a way of reference, the following table is submitted, constructed on the same basis as that on page 81.

TABLE SHOWING THE PRODUCTION OF GOLD AND SILVER, THE PERCENTAGES IN VALUE, THE PROPORTIONS OF WEIGHT, AND THE RESULTING RELATIVE VALUE FROM 1520 TO 1760.

Periods.	Gold. Kilos. Dr. Soetbeer.	Silver. Kilos. Dr. Soetbeer.	Per cent. Value. Gold and Silver.	Proportion of Weight.	Relative Value. Gold and Silver. Dr. Soetbeer.
1521 to 1544	7,160	90,200	56 to 44	1 to 12.4	1 to 11.25
1545 „ 1560	8,510	311,600	29 „ 71	1 „ 37.6	1 „ 11.10
1561 „ 1580	6,840	299,500	26 „ 74	1 „ 43.8	1 „ 11 50
1581 „ 1600	7,380	418,900	21 „ 79	1 „ 56.7	1 „ 11.40
1601 „ 1620	8,520	422,900	24 „ 76	1 „ 49.5	1 „ 12.00
1621 „ 1640	8,300	393,600	25 „ 75	1 „ 47.4	1 „ 14.00
1681 „ 1700	10,765	341,900	33 „ 67	1 „ 31.6	1 „ 14.96
1701 „ 1720	12,820	355,600	36 „ 64	1 „ 27.7	1 „ 15.27
1720 „ 1740	19,080	431,200	41 „ 59	1 „ 22.6	1 „ 15.08
1741 „ 1760	24,610	533,145	42 „ 58	1 „ 21.6	1 „ 14.74

Bearing in mind, now, what has been said as to the causes which led to these fractional differences in decimals, as compared with Dr. Soetbeer's figures here adopted for the relative proportions, and assuming the rate of 1 to 12 as the previous fair basis, it would appear that in spite of the enormous increase in the production of silver between 1521 and 1620, a time of one hundred years, no alteration took place. This flat contradiction of the theory of supply and demand as the only guiding one, occurs in the Table on page 81, and is here further capped by the fact that whereas the value of gold ought to have declined in the time from 1621 to 1760, on account of the increase of production in its turn, it has done the exact contrary.

In order to show what influence the "act of man," or the law, has had upon this result, it must now be stated that as soon as the supplies of silver became heavier in the beginning of the 16th century, the various states commenced to uphold its value by deliberate action. Although no distinct coinage laws were made, the value of current gold coins was determined from time to time by edicts, and in Germany, France,

Spain, and England, for instance, the rate was fixed at from 10.70 to 11.05, and thereabouts. Singular attempts to go much farther were made in England; especially under Henry VIII. and Edward VI., when the rate of 1 to 5 was actually tried. Whether the pressure of law thus had checked the effect of supply or demand, or had an influence quite strong enough without reference to it, its independent force cannot be denied. On the whole the result seems to have been that about the year 1620 the old proportion of 1 to 12 was still prevalent in the majority of states, with such decimal fractions of differences as the nature of coinage and charges of conveyance from one country to another permitted to exist.

But how did the change from 1 to 12 in 1620 to 1 to 15 and thereabouts take place?

The table shows that this change occurred in spite of the enhanced supply of gold, and it follows that the law must again have asserted its power. *Primâ facie* it may be conceded that the law altering coinage proportions must have the actual precedence or the old rules must continue, whether for good or for evil. The law can do nothing absurdly contrary to a reasonable state of things, such as reversing the *rôle* between gold and silver might be. Nor can it operate in isolated national cases inconsistently with the general situation. Thus in the case of the attempts in Rome in 218 B.C. when 1 to 17.0 or in 312 A.D. when 1 to 14.4, were tried, and in 1564 when here in England 1 to 5 was experimented upon, the rest of the world made them all abortive. But when the legislation of the majority of nations tends in the same direction, in the face of supply and demand, the force of that legislation is undoubted.

Now in the sixteenth century the tendency of the proclamations had been in favour of upholding silver in the face of its greater supply. If this tendency was excessive, but successful nevertheless to a certain extent, it is evident that if in the century following it turned towards gold, a similar strongly marked effect would be shown. Then each nation attempted to overreach the other by altering the value of gold, in spite, as it is repeated here, of its greater supply. Owing to the troubles on the continent, England and the Spanish Peninsula, between whom the communication by sea was easier, were chiefly responsible for these legislative vagaries. Spanish, Portuguese, French, and other gold and silver coin were brought to England, or exported, and as the "legal tender" was then not properly defined, even in its elementary meaning, changes took place *ad libitum*.

At last England took a decisive step. The guinea, which had circulated at various rates of from 28 shillings down to 23, was declared at 21 shillings in 1717, both metals being legal tender. No special principle guided the step, it was a mere guess connected with the then debased state of the silver coin current, and that it was "overdone," even as regards this, the sequel proved. The proportion between gold and silver being thus made 1 to 15·21, whilst in Spain, Holland, and elsewhere, it was 1 to 14 and 1 to 14·50, England became denuded of silver. The dearth of silver became so great, that all sorts of inferior foreign and clipped pieces were used. Nor was the rule of 21 English shillings strictly adhered to, for in Ireland in 1737 the guinea was declared 22s. 9d., with a tariff for foreign coins in proportion

Then a second determining step was taken by Spain, outdoing England. In 1730 the Spanish law established the proportion of 1 to 15⅞, taking the Castilian weight division as its foundation. The consequence was that silver returned to England by way of retaliation, and when in 1772 Spain reduced its gold by ¼ carat, and made the proportion 16⅓, the effects of the reimportation of old English and foreign silver into and the export of gold from England became so serious, that in 1774 England limited the legal tender of silver to £25 in any one payment; this being the first time that such an expedient was used for full valued pieces. In 1786 Spain reduced its gold by another half-carat in fineness, making the proportion 1 to 16½. In this struggle between England and Spain other nations participated, but the Spanish extreme effort in 1786 was the last for the moment, for shortly afterwards the French Revolution broke out, England had to adopt a paper valuation, and the matter rested for the time being. In 1804, when the production of silver had again increased, the French adopted the proportion of 1 to 15·5. The traces of the monetary conflict between England and the Peninsula survived in this curious feature, that in the bullion market here the terms "Spanish dollars" and "Portugal gold" were used for quoting prices of the two metals, the latter term continuing until 1816, when "standard gold" was substituted.

This is the simple history of the change of value from 1 to 12 to that of 1 to 15·5 during the last two centuries, the supposition that the varying supply of mines has brought about this result, being altogether contradicted by the facts shown. If it is admitted that gold and silver owe their relative proportions of value to their worth as substance in the first instance, without reference to their use as money, it will be conceded that the great variations in supply ought to have produced greater divergences than are before us. But the comparative regularity of the proportions in former times, modified only by the reasons before given, prove most distinctly that the general agreements produced by the law had its firm influence. The *share of power* which this influence can exercise alongside of the substantial worth and variations in supply can be estimated from the fact, that it kept the relation steady at 1 to 13·3 for 1200 years before 400 B.C., at 1 to 12 for 1900 years, and at 1 to 15·5 for the last 150 years. If the tendency in 1720 had been 1 to 12 and the States had then agreed upon it, it would have been upheld. Gold and silver would have performed their office in intercourse, for the good of creditor and debtor and all other purposes as well as they would now, if the proportions arrived at were supported, instead of being wantonly destroyed by the vagaries of law. It is asserted even that if by universal agreement the nations should decide to adopt a fixed proportion of, say 1 to 8, for instance, and no one could obtain coinage from the mints, excepting at these proportions, the rule could be maintained. Whether under such conditions more gold or more silver would be diverted to other purposes, is a question apart from the abstract correctness of the view. But it is not necessary that we should go so far as this for proving the possibility of maintaining the percentage by the force of law. It is sufficient that the real strength of the rules of supply and demand should be joined by that of the law, so that they may support one another. To rely solely on the simple dry quasi-mathematical conception supposed to be involved in the theory of supply and demand, is as fallacious as the mere reliance on law. Both are unproductive when alone and apart, but engender life and reality when they act in concert.

It was admitted and complained of, that in 1717 the law in England had "overdone" the needful. If it had been more reasonable, silver would not have left the country in such excess, and other nations would not have been obliged to retaliate; the Spanish proceedings in their turn were just as extravagant. Can it be denied that if both had been in better agreement, a more equable state of things would have been the result ? The doctrine, " It is a delusion to believe that the human law can uphold fixed proportions," is therefore wrong in practice as well as in logic. That this doctrine should have been promulgated by English economists in former times when the real causes were not so visible, when it was necessary to find some excuse for the apparent contradiction of legal enactments, is explicable. But now when the confusion under which this doctrine was resorted to has given way to a quicker international understanding, when the experience made during the last thirty years as to the great increase of gold, still more forcibly proves what the human law can do, it is time that both the practical and scientific truth should assert itself.

.

To CHAPTERS I., III. AND XVI.—" *The Controversy.*"

The reader who has not hitherto been acquainted with the general controversy on the subject may have perceived that it is just here in England where the dispute first came to an issue. Inasmuch as that which has here been said seems to imply that England has not followed the right course, it is necessary that the reader should free his mind from all national vanity, so as to be able to judge with impartiality. That this is difficult may be granted, especially as we in England have always been taught that we are the first nation in regard to financial superiority, and are still " wealthy." The greatest difficulty, however, in the way is the extreme doctrinal bigotry with which the majority of our living economists and financial writers still adhere to the gold valuation. How did these doctrines arise ?

The history of the controversy is simply this : from the most remote times to the 18th century gold and silver had served in the manner described, without dispute as to any new theory. In the middle of the last century, however, a discussion arose as to the term " standard," or " measure " of value. In the then embryonic state of economical research this term found great favour, and became a kind of peg upon which a variety of conclusions could be hung. The first of these was the wrong to the creditor, who might be paid in the " cheaper metal." In answer to this it may be said that as the creditor contracts with his debtor upon the same basis that he is paid on, therefore no injury could result to him, for in the contract he can guard against the evil thus fancifully imagined. The one-sided character of the phrase is obvious, and in Chapter XVI. its connection with the word " standard " has been referred to.

Next came the allegation that " gold and silver were always varying in value in accordance with variations of the supply, and that in a country using both metals as legal tender, *the cheaper metal remains and the dearer metal becomes exported.*" This doctrine seemed to be a peculiarly happy one, and it has ever since been the great maxim upon which the previous-mentioned conclusions were based. But what was the real truth ? In the foregoing article on the changes of relative value between gold and silver in England it has been stated, that in 1717 the guinea was declared to be worth 21 shillings in silver, and it was explained why silver left the country. Now this was not due to silver becoming dearer else-where, but to gold being made dearer in England, by force of law. By way of sarcasm almost, the Spanish law turned the tables upon England a few years afterwards, until we had to limit the legal tender of silver to £25. It has never been explained whether by the terms "cheaper" or "dearer" metal, there was meant our own appreciation or that of other States by law, the argument drawn from natural supplies being really against the theory of a general effect rather than for it. Owing to confusion and contradiction, the doctrine nevertheless found great favour, especially as it implied that foreigners were in the habit of trying to take advantage of England, and to this day it is the leading fallacy.

The controversy thus begun in the middle of last century had no practical issue, for, as before stated, England soon after became involved in the French war times. In 1816, however, when the return to specie-payments was contemplated the present gold valuation was adopted. Lord Liverpool represented the doctrines founded on the above-mentioned conceptions so strongly, that they could not be resisted. Besides this, two special points seem to have actuated the legislators of the time. Gold had declined in yield, and England, after the war, had supremacy enough to command the acquisition of it. It is a great question whether gold would have been chosen in 1816, if there had then been any suspicion of the discovery of the Californian and Australian gold mines within less than 40 years afterwards. The other point is that in 1804 the French had adopted the bi-metallic system of 1 to 15.5, and there was so much natural prejudice against them in England that nothing in accord with their proceedings could be done here ; whilst our authorities at the same time well perceived that the French valuation would assist them in acquiring gold against silver.

From 1816 then until 1872 the "equilibrium" described continued undisturbed. In 1858 Cobden translated Chevalier's book, wherein the demonetisation of gold was recommended, and his volume started the re-discussion. Generally here in England, however, during the years of prosperity, the defenders of our gold system even out-did the old economists in their admiration of it. The national pride, the abstract correctness seemingly involved, had intensified the phraseology with which the systems of other nations were made light of. The French system was called the "double," or the "alternative" standard. Although France has since proved itself the country of the greatest financial strength, yet in common talk here its system was declared "unsound." Indeed all the odium that could be thrown upon the bi-metallic system under every form, provided the assertions made would fit in somehow with our current doctrines, was freely heaped on it. This ultimately extended its influence to France and Germany; and if France had conquered in the war of 1870-71 there is no doubt that Napoleon III. would have employed the war indemnity he hoped to extract from the vanquished for the purpose of changing the French valuation. The present writer can give proof that this was the intention of the French Government at the time when the Imperial Commission on the question was held in March 1870. It so happened, however, that the Germans turned the tables upon France.

The upsetting of the equilibrium and all the consequences thereof, which have here been fully described, followed upon this, and the question now is—Will England act in the right direction ? Many people who have carefully read this book, may think that this should be done, and considering the attitude which the present

Premier took in 1873 and recently, together with the movements in favour of inquiry now made by merchants and others, will deem this likely. But they must be told that the majority of our English economists and financial newspapers still adhere to the absolute supremacy of our system, and use the same old phrases in its defence. There are well known members of Parliament who will oppose any inquiry into the subject. Efforts are made in learned and other meetings to attribute the depression to all other sorts of causes, except to the one here before us. At the Statistical Society's meeting of the 1st April, 1879, one lecturer endeavours to show that there is a "sufficiency of gold," in spite of the decline in its production. As to the systems of valuations in silver among the majority of nations, and the existing basis of contract (See page 19), he is absolutely silent, for the simple reason that he knows nothing whatever about this part of the matter. Professor Jevons (See page 82) looks upon enquiry into the question of silver with supreme contempt. He is of the opinion that the evils of the time are connected with the spots in the sun,* that England must resign itself to its fate. It is to be hoped that there are Englishmen of greater faith in earthly matters, and of better courage. The President of the meeting, Mr. Shaw Lefevre, M.P., is so much under the influence of the insufficient theory of supply and demand, the wrong of which has been shown on pages 81 and 82, that he cannot refrain from saying, "anybody venturing to introduce bi-metallism here is almost worthy of a place in a lunatic asylum." The reader must decide whether in these pages representing the bi-metallic views, there is anything so contrary to common sense, or in the more comprehensive theory of supply and demand anything so unscientific, as to justify the fanatic attitude adopted by Mr. Shaw Leferve and his consorts.

During the discussion on the Indian Budget, which took place in the House of Commons on the 12th June 1879, the Right Hon. J. G. Hubbard made the following remarks quoted from the report in the *Times :*—

One of the plans suggested by which to improve the existing state of things was that of a double standard, more properly called an alternative standard. Another plan had also been invented called the bi-metallic system, and bi-metallism had been preached as a doctrine by a variety of distinguished men. It had been remarked that this scheme was entirely free from the inconvenience attaching to a double standard, because, whereas this inconvenience consisted in the fact that one or other of the two standards was always varying in value, under a bi-metallic system the standards must always remain of the same value. The bi-metallic system, however, involved the necessity of all countries—at all events those within the circle of civilization—combining to determine that gold and silver should relatively to each other have a certain defined proportionate value. If we had such a system in this country, any amount of silver or any amount of gold might always be introduced and lodged to the credit of the importer at precisely the rate fixed by this cosmopolitan convention. But it would never be possible to obtain from the nations of the world the *consensus* required before a bi-metallic system could be established. If its establishment were possible, however, what would be the result in England? Why, supposing a Mexican were to discover an exceedingly rich mine and be able to produce an enormous amount of silver at a shilling an ounce, he would have a right to send it to this country and have it carried to his account at the contract price, which might be 5s. per ounce. The consequence would be that the amount of currency of gold and silver would be so much enlarged that the whole of it would deteriorate in value. Neither the alternative standard system nor the bi-metallic system could be adopted in this country if we possessed any reasonable regard for our own interests. . . . . . If he were to be asked what should be done in the present state of affairs, he should frankly answer that he did not know what could be done to remedy the irremediable, &c., &c."

The constant repetition of the terms "double" or "alternative" standard, with its allusion to bimetallism as something different, here again prevailed. The

---

* The sunspot theory is one of the latest refuges to which the monometallic party have recourse at this time. No one denies that the sunspots have an influence on the weather, and the weather an effect on the harvests. But, excepting in the case of actual national famines, the price of corn does not now play the *rôle* it did formerly. At all events, the old habit of bygone economists of connecting it with the "valuation" as the guiding factor ought now to give way to the reality of what is involved in social life. Neither the commercial crises, nor the long continued depression of trade at this time have anything to do with the sun. But it is not to be wondered at, that when an economist induces other people to stare at its light, the faculty of observing what goes on on earth becomes much impaired.

problematical fear of "Mexico" producing silver at one shilling an ounce, and swamping England with it, again shows the old bugbear raised by the gold party, to frighten themselves and the public. Mr. Hubbard may be told that many an ounce of gold even has been produced at a cost of no more than five shillings an ounce, and yet has been received in England at 77 shillings for the world's benefit. His terror in regard to the danger with which England's circulation is supposed to be thus threatened, is surpassed only by the error involved in his reference to the interests of England. Like the rest of the gold advocates, he has nothing to show as regards this interest, except his own assertion ; but it may strike many people that in the book before them fair evidence has been given that the interests of England lie in the direction of the use of silver. It cannot be expected that gentlemen of the type of Mr. Hubbard, who for a lifetime have taken a leading part in maintaining the ruling doctrines of the time, will at once consent to their revision, even when the signs of distress are so pressing. But if people in such responsible positions, when they are asked what should be done in the present state of affairs, and can only answer that "they do not know how to remedy the irremediable," does it follow that the British public bow meekly to this finale of wisdom ? The responsibility which some doubtless eminent men load upon themselves in thus refusing every recognition to the strongest facts brought before them, rather than sacrifice one iota of their old dogmatic creeds, is serious ; the hope may be expressed that true patriotism will rescue the country from the consequences.

The following are a few specimens of passages from newspaper paragraphs and letters. One powerful daily paper, alluding to the Indian difficulty, said lately :—

"For the relief of that trade, if nothing else, India will have, sooner or later, to borrow in this market, and that to a very large amount. An estimated further drop of 1½ per cent. in the exchanges of the current year is something which cannot be passed over with the mere observation that the change in the relative value of gold and silver has alone disturbed the satisfactory financial condition of India, and that this is under the consideration of the Home Government. This observation seems to point to the trial of some nostrum for 'restoring' silver and gold to their normal relative values, and the actual state of the case makes such an idea all the more to be regretted. There could be no greater fallacy than that embodied in most of the currency nostrums in vogue, and should India rest her financial salvation on any of them her dangers will multiply. The true cause of depressed exchanges is the superabundance of Council drafts, and till India can reduce her expenses she must borrow here. Relief can come in no other way ; least of all by efforts to force her silver on European markets at a fancy price."

The misconception as to the Indian Council drafts may appear from what has here been said on page 64. The characteristic of this style of thing is in the expression "nostrum" so often used instead of reasoning.

A deputation of the Liverpool Chamber of Commerce, convinced of the true cause of the depression, having waited upon the Chancellor of the Exchequer to urge the remonetisation of silver, a weekly financial paper on the 12th April, 1879, said :—

A deputation from the Liverpool Chamber of Commerce waited upon the Chancellor of the Exchequer at the end of last week to urge upon the Cabinet to invite an international conference, with a view to the universal adoption of bi-metallism. The United States Government invited such a conference last summer, and its experience is not calculated to encourage Ministers to repeat the experiment. Germany will have nothing to do with nostrums of the kind, and, therefore, universal bi-metallism is out of the question. For the rest, the Chancellor of the Exchequer gave little encouragement to the proposal to tamper with the currency. It is surprising that arguments such as were put forward by this deputation can impose upon sensible men of business. There is not a tittle of proof that the depreciation of silver has in any way contributed to the badness of any trade but the Eastern, and that is adversely affected by so many causes that it is impossible to say for how much depreciation counts. In any case, it is so small a part of the whole trade of the country that it would be folly to abandon a good monetary system because of it. As for the apprehensions expressed of general demonetisation of silver and a ruinous fall of prices, they are mere fantasies. General demonetisation is too costly to be carried out, and nobody has attempted to prove that a permanently lower level of prices would be injurious.

The writer has no idea that the demonetisation by France and other nations is not a matter of choice, and that the expense supposed to be involved, whatever it may be, is of less moment than that incurred in consequence of the present state of things. (See page 96).

Another influential monetary paper says :—

We have been curious to see how these resolutions of the Liverpool Chamber would be taken in India, a country which has the largest possible inducement next to the silver-producing countries, in seeing silver appreciated and protected at the expense of gold depreciated and attacked. It is, therefore, with much interest that we have read an article in the columns of our able contemporary in Calcutta, the *Englishman*, of April 24th. It condemns the resolutions of the Liverpool Chamber as arising from a delusion which, in some unaccountable way, seems to have got hold of the Liverpool merchants that the effect of declaring silver to be worth so much more in relation to gold, would be that the world's monetary wealth would be correspondingly increased ; and it marvels at the fact that, after all that has been said and written on the subject, from the days of Adam Smith to our own, such a belief can have been entertained.

All who know the real nature of the case are aware that this is not a question of attacking gold, as the article puts it. The expression "delusion," as applied to the merchants of Liverpool, among whom are men of as high an education as can be found in this country, and of far greater foresight and experience in the commerce of the world than could ever be found in an editorial chair, again betrays the character of the monometallic bigotry. The allusion to Adam Smith, whom we all respect, shows the want of original power of thought under which so many of our economists are labouring. Adam Smith wrote just at the time when the struggle between the English and Spanish laws were going on, and when the doctrines then stated were peculiarly acceptable to the British public. (See pages 85 to 87.)

The object in view of here calling attention to these more or less fierce attacks on the remonetisation of silver is that of acquainting the reader not yet initiated into the controversy with their nature. They will appear over and over again in similar tones, or in a more deliberate form with a kind of quasi-scientific aspect founded upon the old doctrines. In one of these quasi-scientific articles defending the current conceptions the following conclusion appeared :—

"This country adopted the gold valuation according to the principles laid down by Lord Liverpool and others before him. Every experience since has only convinced us that we were right in doing this, and nobody has as yet proved that the present depression of trade can be connected with that policy."

May it not be claimed that in the book now before the reader this connection has been sufficiently established? The fact is that the writers in favour of the gold valuation make "assertions of principles," but have never supported them by intelligible statistics, with the exception of the returns of our increasing commerce, and this resource has now failed on account of the continuous decline.

Whilst the advocates of the gold valuation thus had no tangible grounds for insisting on its advantages, it may be stated that the writers opposing them clearly foresaw the distressing result on trade we are now witnessing. Even early in this century some of our economists spoke in favour of the maintenance of the concurrent use of gold and silver. But as the equilibrium established in 1816 did not cause an international disturbance, their views had little influence. Our statesmen of 1816 well recognised that the gold valuation was to be adopted for England, because it seemed to suit at the time ; none of them thought of abusing the systems of other nations ; far less were they inclined to recommend that other nations should also adopt our system. The fanatical tendency to do this was reserved for the modern school, who thereby destroyed the supposed advantage of England's position. The controversy, therefore, became intense only when in 1867 the French showed a disposition to follow England's example; and from this time the more violent struggle set in; those in favour of the use of silver alongside of gold warning the world against the extension of the gold valuation.

In a book issued in 1868*, the writer first stated the outlines of the views here represented. The late Senator Wolowski, of France, who may truly be called the father of bi-metallism, translated portions of the same in his work on the subject. In another publication, issued in 1869†, those views were more specially affirmed. In 1876, when the fall in the price of silver created some alarm, the author read a paper‡, and in 1878 he again followed up the subject, before the Society of Arts.§ In all these publications it was distinctly stated that the demonetisation of silver was the orginal cause of the decline of trade. In 1871 the writer ventured to say :—

"It is a great mistake to suppose that the adoption of the gold valuation by other States besides England will be beneficial. It will only lead to the destruction of the monetary equilibrium hitherto existing and cause a fall in the value of silver, from which England's trade and the Indian silver valuation will suffer more than all other interests, grievous as the general decline of prosperity all over the world will be. The strong doctrinism existing in England as regards the gold valuation is so blind, that when the time of depression sets in, there will be this especial feature : the economical authorities of the country will refuse to listen to the cause here foreshadowed, every possible attempt will be made to prove that the decline of commerce is due to all sorts of causes and irreconcilable matters. The workman and his strikes will be the first convenient target; then speculation and overtrading will have their turn. Later on, when foreign nations, unable to pay in silver, have recourse to protection, when a number of other secondary causes develope themselves, then many would-be wise men will have the opportunity of pointing to specific reasons which in their eyes account for the falling off in every branch of trade. Many other allegations will be made, totally irrelevant to the real issue, but satisfactory to the moralising tendency of financial writers. The great danger of the time will then be, that among all this confusion and strife, England's supremacy in commerce and manufacture may go backwards to an extent which cannot be redressed when the real cause becomes recognised and the natural remedy is applied." ·

The *rôle* of a prophet is not a desirable one, and these remarks are only quoted to show that the views held by bi-metallists have been confirmed by events. But, besides the writer of these pages, there are numerous other authorities here and abroad, amongst whom Monsieur Henri Cernuschi (the spirited inventor of the word "bi-metallism"), requires special mention, who agree with the opinions here expressed.

Throughout the country and abroad, the necessity of preventing the further spread of the misfortunes due to this cause is beginning to be recognised. Besides the Liverpool Chamber of Commerce and others, a number of international bankers and merchants of London of the highest position have petitioned the Government to institute enquiry into the subject. The Government have admitted the importance of these representations, and promised to give attention to them. It lies in the power of the British public to assist them, by refusing to give countenance to the uncompromising language with which some of the organs of the press treat the question. It may, at least, be hoped that the material furnished in this book will supply statements and reasons which may enable the reader to detect where are the cloven feet in the controversy.

* "Bullion and Foreign Exchanges." 700 pp. Effingham Wilson. 1868.

† ' The Depreciation of Labour and Property which would follow the Demonetisation of Silver." 109 pp. Effingham Wilson. 1869.

‡ "The Fall in the Price of Silver." 112 pp. H. S. King and Co. 1876.

§ The Wealth of Nations, and the Question of Silver." Eden Fisher and Co., 50 Lombard Street. 551 pp.

To Chapter I.—*The Interest of all Classes in the Question.*

It will now be intelligible, why in the first Chapter, so earnest an appeal has been made to all classes, to endeavour to form a correct judgment on the question. The hindrances to a true appreciation of it have been pointed out, and it must be obvious, that unless public opinion encourage the Government to take action, the mischief will increase. There is not one single class in the country, that is not interested in the remonetisation of silver, but unfortunately, there are a few persons who imagine that they derive advantage from the existing situation, viz.: salaried officials and a few capitalists who hope to profit by the low prices already current, and which must sink still lower. It is hardly necessary to expose the fallacy of their creed, for the capitalist and official must share in the general welfare or disaster of the community; the man who has money to employ, may still find bargains, but a universal decline in prosperity will ultimately deprive him of this advantage. It is however, a noteworthy fact, that in the present controversy, the writers who advocate a single gold standard belong principally to the salaried class, and although their motives may be most disinterested, it cannot be forgotten that personal interest is a powerful, though very often an unconscious, factor in the propounding of theories.

The welfare of all persons with variable incomes: landowners, bankers, merchants, shipowners, manufacturers and the entire labouring population, is dependent on a clear apprehension of the silver question, and a sound conclusion respecting it. For the moment, it seems as if their interests were threatened as though by the hand of fate, but as a matter of fact, what is called fate, is but folly in regard to legislation affecting money, and can be set right by the application of good sense and correct science.

The *landowner*, finding that his farm rents are falling off, and that his income is vanishing, accepts the current explanation that America and other countries are sending us corn and meat, at prices with which English farmers cannot compete. But if these rivals in the provision market could send us silver, as was open to them to do previous to 1872, they would not only take more goods from us, but being in this way, profitable customers, they would increase our capacity for home consumption. That the severe competition complained of should date from 1872 confirms the view that if the old position of the precious metals were restored, the old prosperity would be regained and exceeded. The *landowner* must not, however, regard the struggle from a merely selfish point of view; his prosperity is bound up with, if it does does not depend on, the commercial interests of the country, and it is for him to make common cause with them.

Owners of property in houses, buildings, etc., have not as yet felt the growing depression severely, but the decline in value of their investments has already set in and must continue. *Investors in industrial undertakings* are losing heavily, while much of the capital devoted to other schemes must be looked upon as entirely lost. *The banking interests* are likewise threatened, because, for obvious reasons the number of securities in their hands on now depreciated land and property have vastly increased, while their implication in the losing industry and commerce of the Empire is deepening.

To manufacturers the question is one of life or death. Upon their success and profits the financial strength of England mainly depends. Let them ask why it is that our exports have sustained so marked a check since 1873 ? Why have the natural benefits of free trade have been so suddenly lost ? It is said, that foreign competition and protective duties have caused it, but an examination of the facts shows that such assertions are mere subterfuges. One innocent occurrence after another has been charged with causing the present depression, from the exhibition of 1851 down to the existence of a Conservative Government. Have the Associated Chambers of Commerce nothing to give us but explanations which would not deceive a child ? Can Manchester, when veritably in a struggle for existence, find comfort in the few poor and illogical platitudes uttered by the Gold party? Happily, the merchants of London and Liverpool, as represented by their ablest spokesmen, have shown that they appreciate the gravity of the situation, and are not to be lulled into a false security by the cry, "peace, peace, when there is no peace." Many of them, specially the large and influential section who do business with silver-using markets, know very well what is the matter, and are aware that before the commerce of the country and of the world can revive, the currency question must be grappled with by statesmen and settled for generations.

From *professional freetraders*, by whom are meant, for instance, members of the Cobden Club, the subject demands earnest attention, for it was Cobden that translated Chevalier's book in 1858, hinting at the demonetisation of *gold*, and the existing phase of the controversy makes the inconsistent conduct of Chevalier conspicuous. The club took an interest in the Paris conference, and it is now wondered whether their leaders are content to be mere bottleholders. They should speak *now*, or for ever hold their peace, for the tendency toward protective duties, or perhaps it should be said, the necessity laid upon foreign nations of protecting their industries, is due to the demonetisation of silver. People who misunderstand the question, say, "Everyone may trade in silver if he pleases," but they are altogether misled, because the gold valuation practically forbids trade in silver coin as legal tender. It is the province and the duty of the State to coin gold and silver for the facility of trade, and the moment this free coinage is refused, the principles of free trade are outraged and the commerce of the nation is hampered. Unless these evils are remedied, the annual dinners at the Cobden Club, will, in future, give less and less occasion for mutual congratulations.

Commerce *cannot suffer alone*. In striking at it, you strike at the centre, at the heart of national prosperity, and from one extremity of the body corporate to the other, the effect is felt. The trader's profits are gone, and what can become of the multitude who live upon those profits ? Hence it is that literary men, artists and all, the products of whose brains are among the commodities of highly civilised States, must share the existing depression, and that they do share it, a visit to Christie and Manson, or a commission of enquiry into the secrets of Paternoster row, will prove. Are they to bear their loss in silence, and will they not join in a demand for inquiry into this question concerning money, now that it is placed before them in a reasonable form ? What is so regrettable is, that all the great advance in civilisation and art, all the natural right of mankind thereto should thus be forcibly curtailed by no other power than the obstinacy of a few leading financiers, and their blind, badly tutored adherents. Of the fallacies of this tutoring the statements in Chapter 16, page 36, and Appendix, page 81, are examples of the most striking nature.

Go further, to the extremities of this body corporate of England—to *the vast labouring population*, and can it be believed that their representatives, such men as Butt, Macdonald, Howell, Potter, Arch, and others, will give themselves no trouble to understand this question, and if need be to insist on its proper settlement? That a great deal of the strife for life is the result of the depression in trade, they will be the first to admit, but do they realise how much of the bitterness of the struggle between capital and labour would be done away with, if the injurious restrictions upon currency were abolished? No question of class legislation can be raised, for the establishment of a sound silver currency for the people could result only in advantage to them and still more to the classes above them.

What are our *philanthropists* going to do in this matter? By taking the right side, they may remove many a social incongruity, and bring about not merely national prosperity, but the recognition of some plain practical truths. Will they not plead on behalf of the people? There is many a poor fellow thrown out of work by "the bad times" who walks gloomily about the street, unable to obtain work from his master, and without change which would enable him to pass his own handicraft work to anyone in a position to use it. Suffering comes on him, and then its twin sister, vice, follows, and what is your *philanthropy* doing? Can it do nothing more than "repress mendicity" and suggest the workhouse or emigration? Your "*learned professors*," are they able only to tabulate statistics of drunkenness, strikes and crime, furnishing weapons with which less gifted minds may attack the "inferior classes."

Is there not a more noble school of men who, coming to this controversy with minds untrammelled by prejudice, will give to the facts which have been put forth in this treatise the attention which they deserve, and in doing so will feel as a number of others have already felt, that a new revelation has opened to them? If it be so, let them not be satisfied with a tacit assent to the views usually advocated, but let them come forward and join those who are determined that the authorities of the country shall have no rest until right has been done to the people.

The reputation of the nation and of its rulers for economical intelligence and practical sense is at stake.

All who recognise the cause of the existing depression must admit, that if England takes her proper place in assisting in a remonetisation of silver, the gloom which now hangs over the land will pass away. On the other hand, if nothing is done, if it be supposed that the natural course of trade will "somehow set it right," this *laisser faire* policy, this happy-go-lucky administration of affairs, will bring about disaster, and bring it chiefly upon England.

The losses already incurred, and now being incurred, in trade may not improbably bring about a crisis without parallel. But that will not be the end of the mischief. In proportion as we compel foreign states to manufacture for themselves, and increase their protective duties, the legitimate trade of this country will further fall off, and the steady downward course of its Empire will have been entered upon. Periods of spasmodic improvement may occur, and lull into false confidence the popular optimists of the day, but if the wound be not cured before it be too late, the lapse of a few years may give Englishmen sad cause to regret that the commercial supremacy of England was sacrificed because an exclusively national theory prevented their recognition of the truth.

ADDITIONAL.

The prospective Demonetisation of Silver by France and the Latin Union.

Since writing this book the author has been asked to define more distinctly the reasons on which he founds his assertion that other nations, France, for instance, will be compelled to demonetise silver. (See Chapter VII. p. 14.) It appears that the chief effect of the demonetisation, namely the enforced cessation of the further coinage of silver by the bi-metallic states, such as France, is now being recognised as the chief cause of the fall in the value of that metal. Nevertheless, it is asked, "Why should not France and the other bi-metallic countries keep the silver they now hold at its depreciated value?" This suggestion is supported by the assertion, that "demonetisation would be too expensive for France." It is upon such a weak foundation that some of our statesmen, Mr. Goschen among them, seem to rely, in the hope of postponing the consideration of the danger with which India is threatened. And others recommend that we should wait, on the ground that matters will come right at last by themselves.

Does anyone doubt that France could make a very heavy monetary sacrifice if it were required? To place this matter on a basis which does not merely involve the *ex cathedrâ* command which English economists are so fond of addressing to foreign nations, but which concerns our own interest, and is therefore subjected by us to more careful consideration, let the question be asked, "What would England or India give in a round sum, if the latter country could exchange her silver for gold?" If India had had a gold currency all the losses already incurred would not have happened. The loss of value in the total Indian silver currency, the losses in commerce, and in incomes, which might be capitalized, can be set aside. But dealing only with the annual loss suffered by the Indian Government of £3 to £4 millions, which loss is *absolute*, from which no one gains, and which may continue for an indefinite time, would, or should, our Government hesitate to sacrifice, say, £10 millions in a lump sum, in order to set this matter at rest for ever? Let Indian statesmen and financiers answer this question. Now, as far as India is concerned, the continued depreciation of her currency is serious enough. Whether this depreciation is increased by the forcible injection into India of more silver by loans raised here until India sickens with it (See p. 67), is so far but a simple matter. She is free at all events from the danger of the introduction of rupees by private coinage, for the operation would not pay. Her chief danger arises from the probability of her being swamped with silver as a result of the prospective demonetisation of that metal in France.

And it is just in regard to this prospective demonetisation of silver that the position of France is so entirely different. Without reference to the reasons given in Chapter VII., it can easily be shown why France *must* demonetise silver, unless its price be restored by an international understanding.

The Government of France is responsible for the value of the 5 franc silver piece. Its full legal tender rights cannot be abrogated unless the French Government provides for their redemption at full value. Until such a step is taken the Government, the Bank, and the public are bound to receive the 5 franc pieces in payment to any amount. Now the French Government *cannot for any length of time retain these pieces in circulation* if the market price of silver continues to leave so large a margin as at present on the private coinage of 5 franc silver pieces. It has been explained in Chapter II., and Appendix page 59, that our subsidiary silver coinage is less liable to this danger, because its tender is limited to £2 in any one payment; and since even here operations of this kind might be conducted profitably when the price of silver is sufficiently low, a much less margin between the market price and the mint price would suffice in the case of full legal tender coins, such as these 5 franc pieces. Such full legal tender silver coins can be disposed of to any amount, and there is absolutely no possibility of distinguishing between coins issued by the mint and by private persons, when once they are put in circulation. Considering that not only in Germany, but in France and other bi-metallic States this process might go on indefinitely, it is evident that the position forms a Gordian knot, which can only be severed by the demonetising and melting down of the whole legal tender silver coinage of these countries. The French Government, for instance, would be compelled to assign a period after which the 5 fr. piece would be declared "*hors cours.*" During this period of, say, one or two years, the surreptitious coinage would have to be endured. The stock of silver held by the Government would of course be sold at once for what it would bring, for the pieces forming it could not again be put in circulation, and would have to be melted by the State.

It is somewhat surprising that in England, where we are so well aware of the importance of the cardinal rule, that the real should be identical with the nominal value of legal tender coins, there are people who expect that foreign nations will act on different principles. In France especially, where full valued metallic currency is even more firmly rooted in the minds of the people than in England, it would be less possible to maintain such an anomaly than anywhere else.

But there is a still more cogent reason for the necessity of France's clearing the ground on which she stands at whatever cost it may be. The continued circulation of her silver coinage at a depreciated value, even if it amount to only one-third of the total circulation, or if such silver is held against note issue by the Bank of France, is equivalent to a depreciation of the entire currency, and therefore entails all the evils of such a state of things. It would lead to an inflation of prices, thus weakening the exporting power of the country, and unduly promoting the imports. The resulting loss of her balance of trade would be so considerable that France would do better to sacrifice her entire silver currency once for all. To show how powerful a force France has exerted by her balance of trade, it may be mentioned, that although she paid away £200 millions from 1871 to 1874, yet she has since regained the whole of what she then parted with by sheer force of industry. It is altogether a narrow-minded idea to suppose that this matter concerns a mere sacrifice in currency. As has been shewn in Appendix, p. 53, we in England have already lost more than double the amount of our entire currency by the loss in our trade which the demonetisation of silver has indirectly brought about.

A more forcible illustration of the real principle involved is furnished by the United States of America. Scarcely ten years ago, the balance of trade against the United

States was £40 millions per annum; it is now more than £40 millions in their favour. How has this variation of £80 millions been brought about in so short a time? The answer is: By the strict adherence of the American Government to the principle of limiting the paper circulation, in spite of increasing population and the clamours of the greenback party, until the present parity of the legal tender notes to the gold basis has been reached. The low prices produced by this policy checked foreign importation, encouraged the export of American produce, forced the people to increased industry, and to engage in the competition with our own manufacturers, which we now have to expect. If the Americans were to give way to the silver party without an international understanding, and so create a redundancy of silver currency at home, they would again so inflate prices as to lose their balance of trade. The present production of silver in the United States, is from £6 to £8 millions annually. The balance of trade in their favour is £40 millions. Now, if this prudent action of America in regard to currency has produced so wonderful a change in the economic condition of the United States, seeing that greenbacks are now at par with gold, it would be monstrous folly on the part of America to substitute an internationally depreciated currency in the place of the more valuable greenbacks. The silver party in the United States may lose, say, half of the value of their present silver, or about £3 or £4 millions per annum, but the nation would retain the £40 millions of balance of trade in their favour, with a prospect of its increase. Statesmen in America are well aware of this, and know that if the silver party succeeds even in bringing about some enforced arrangement, it will speedily break down. The American Government as yet holds the silver dollars in abeyance in the Treasury, for fear of losing its stock of gold and the power of maintaining the gold basis thus gained. On our part it is foolish to rely upon the absorption of the American silver by the Americans themselves, as Mr. Goschen does, as it is altogether ludicrous for us to expect other nations to commit blunders in order to benefit us. The true principles involved in this will assert themselves with unfailing force, and it is astounding to notice that English statesmen and financiers appear to hold "foreign nations," as beyond the pale of their influence. That statesmen in France or America have not yet initiated definite action in these matters is probably due to the more or less chaotic state of opinion under which they, as well as our own financial authorities, are labouring. We watch them in the hope that they will pull the chesnuts out of the fire for us. They watch us in the hope that we shall become more reasonable. But they have this advantage over us, that, since they are now forced *nolens volens* to foster home industry in order to emancipate themselves from us, they will before long gain a position of independence, which may result in the state of things alluded to in Chapter X., p. 23, in the following words, " It is not impossible that, under all the circumstances, England and India will be stranded together on the silver basis itself."

All the warfare thus engendered by the momentary situation, the necessity under which nations labour for lowering the value of commodities, in order to avoid national inflation, are but the consequences of the unintelligent policy of England. Were English statesmen active in this cause, were gold and silver restored to their proper position by the only means now open, namely, a general international agreement, all this conflict would speedily cease. Instead of the present rivalry in prices, the general beneficent rise by the equal distribution of the increased metallic means of exchange would place matters in the world upon quite a different footing. All nations would derive advantage from it, but England especially, because her industry has a kind of prescriptive right to its superiority.

As regards this question of the prospective demonetisation of silver by France and other bi-metallic states, which is likely to further endanger India, no one in his senses could advise France and the United States to adhere to bi-metallism under the present circumstances. If the international understanding cannot be come to, the advocates of the gold valuation in France and elsewhere are absolutely in their right when they insist upon saying that the surrender of the entire silver currency is preferable to the present uncertain state of things and the annual drawback which the depreciation entails upon them. France will not hesitate to sacrifice £40, or £50 millions or more, if necessary, to protect herself. The situation, as well as the advocates of the gold system, are now preparing her for this necessity; the obstinacy of Germany may then be rivalled by France, and both may treat us with the same disregard with which we have hitherto treated them. Let it be recollected that in saying this the question of the merits or demerits of the gold valuation is not before us, but the issue only of the further danger threatening India by the prospective demonetisation of silver in France. If our statesmen contemplate waiting until foreign countries can no longer resist, and preparations in secret are made; until the respective laws to be promulgated by France and other states pass from their condition of preliminary consideration to definite "Bills" before the Legislature, it will already be too late. The passage of such laws is a matter of a moment, and will change the aspect of the situation in a twinkling, regardless of consequences.

That the unerring force of certain true maxims of monetary science should be deemed inapplicable to France and other countries, in excuse for our procrastination, is something like the folly of the ostrich, who purposely buries his head in the sand in order not to see the rapidly approaching enemy. Many of the statesmen financiers of England of the present time—seem to be unable to understand the real position. One of them imagines that Germany, having spent a large amount for gold, will now recur to the bi-metallic system. If Germany did this, it is evident that France, for instance, would immediately exchange her stock of silver for German gold. Without an international agreement between Germany and France this could not be prevented. But even if France, Germany, the United States and other countries positively agreed to a mutual arrangement, that arrangement would have no chance of success, unless England and India were not inimical to it; and England and India *must* be inimical to it unless they join it. (See Chapter XV.)

It will be obvious to all who really understand the situation, that *the present depressed condition of England's trade is quite serious enough without reference to the prospective demonetisation of silver by France.* What England requires, and her men of business desire, is to be relieved from *the present ruinous and uncertain state of matters, which calls for help, and not to be requested to wait* until the adoption of the policy enforced on France renders the *situation still more intolerable and ruinous.* Even if the vague hopes of our statesmen that something will occur to raise the price of silver, or that France will not demonetise, were better founded than they are, their present attitude displays a want of foresight and power to perceive facts, which is hardly credible. It implies a failure to grasp the realities of a position, which is quite independent of the rights or wrongs of the controversy regarding the system of valuation. The bygone economists of this country, dogmatical as some of them were, had had a more lively sense of the international aspects of monetary matters and of their importance as regards the interests of this country.

It is the British empire especially which holds the largest stock of silver. (See Chapter X., page 22.) It is England herself which has the greatest interest in the maintenance of that metal as a legal means of exchange in the world's trade. (See Chapter XI. and Appendix page 47.) England at this moment requires leaders which can see this in spite of such weak assumptions as the one here pointed out, and energetic men who will not be content with the current refuge for the destitute economist: that of leaving things to set themselves right. The theory of supply and demand has its unquestionable force, but it is an insult to that very theory to deny that legislation is a factor which must be taken into account. Our legislature has passed monetary laws with the express object of exercising an influence on the value of the precious metals, and nothing can be more inconsistent than the optimistic indolence of those who are in favour of leaving the whole thing to chance for all aftertimes.

It is believed by many people that the present time is a favourable one for the success of another international conference. Germany abstained from the last, for in the first flush of her pride in its gold-valuation she was still obstinate; but since then, as the speeches of Bismarck show, some change of opinion as to the expediency of the system has been manifested. As stated before, Germany will not lay itself open to the play on the bi-metallic valuation resulting from the opposing English and Indian systems, but she seems inclined to retain a sufficient number of thalers for internal circulation. If therefore our Government were willing (See Chapter XX.) to co-operate by coining four-shilling pieces under the restricted tender as proposed, the Germans might be willing to adopt the same kind of preliminary compromise. But it stands to reason that such an agreement must be attempted very soon, for in the rapidly changing condition of things any further delay will increase the difficulties of a proper reconciliation and ultimately render it impossible.

INDEX.

Civil Service Printing and Publishing Company Limited, 8 Salisbury Court, Fleet Street, London, E.C.